food adventures

food adventures

introducing your child to flavours from around the world

Elisabeth Luard & Frances Boswell

photography by Ngoc Minh Ngo

KYLE CATHIE LIMITED

For Jessie, Bonnie, Sophie, Harper,
Beatriz Plum, Iona and Little Brother Orin,
without whom there would have been no book.

First published in Great Britain in 2006 by
KYLE CATHIE LIMITED
122 Arlington Road
London NW1 7HP
general.enquiries@kyle-cathie.com
www.kylecathie.com

ISBN (10-digit) 1 85626 667 2
ISBN (13-digit) 978 1 85626 667 3

Project editor CAROLINE TAGGART
Copy editor MORAG LYALL
Index by ANNA NORMAN
Production by SHA HUXTABLE and ALICE HOLLOWAY

Elisabeth Luard and Frances Boswell are hereby identified as the author of this work
in accordance with Section 77 of the Copyright, Designs and Patents Act 1988.

A Cataloguing in Publication record for this title is available from the British Library.

Printed in Singapore by Star Standard

introduction 6

1 first real food 11
purées and broths 12, bowl food 17, first aid 23

2 window of opportunity 29

3 join the gang 39

4 life's a game 63

5 sniff 'n' seek 75

6 the takeaway trick 89

7 the restaurant table 105

8 cooking together 121

9 off to school 139

index 158 / acknowledgements 160 / conversion tables 160

Ten fingers, ten toes. Check. New life on the planet.

The arrival of a first baby is the moment of truth in any adult relationship. Anyone can fall in love, marry or not. But a baby is something else. It's a joy, naturally, and a responsibility. But it's also earth-shattering, the bolt of lightning which changes the world for ever.

New life needs to eat. And the choice is yours. But all over the world, people who live in multi-generational households don't reach for the packet or open the jar. Instead, they feed their babies a little of what they themselves eat, in easily digested form — a practice made possible because someone else is helping around the house. Few of us have such luxury. But most of us do have times — weekends, holidays, even weekday evenings — when cooking is perfectly possible. The aim of this book is to make those times a pleasure rather than a chore.

As members of an extended family, Frances and I — daughter-in-law and mother-in-law — are aware of how much we need each other, trading advice, support and even, at times, transatlantic babysitting. Happily, we share

an interest – more than that, a career, since it's the way we both earn our living. We write about food: how it looks, where it comes from, how to make it taste good. Which is not to say we live our lives in exactly the same way. We cook differently, just as we parent differently, and our relationship is all the more valuable because we learn from each other. One of us is naturally innovative, unafraid to substitute an ingredient or present a dish in a new way; the other is instinctively traditional, always looking for the story behind the story, needing to know exactly why the cooks of Portugal have a taste for fresh coriander or the Chinese serve sweet things along with the soup. No prizes for guessing which is which. But we never disagree on the

basics: that food should taste good because it *is* good, and that this is a lesson you're never too young to learn.

Our testers, the dedicatees of this book – their ages ranging from 3 months to 7 years old – didn't like everything we put in front of them. By no means. But they did try everything at least once. And it certainly helped that we knew the food tasted delicious, because we'd tried it ourselves, applying the same standards as we would to any dish we cooked for friends and family. Our children's relationship with food is important to both of us, just as food is important in our relationship with each other.

All the recipes in this book are what the inhabitants of at least one corner of the world consider a normal, healthy diet for their youngsters. None of them will seem more than a little bit exotic since most are familiar if not from travel, then from restaurant menus. Ingredients are mostly what can be picked up at your local store; if they're not we take care to suggest alternatives.

So here we are. The fire's lit. The door's open. Come right in and make yourselves at home.

ELISABETH LUARD
MAY 2006

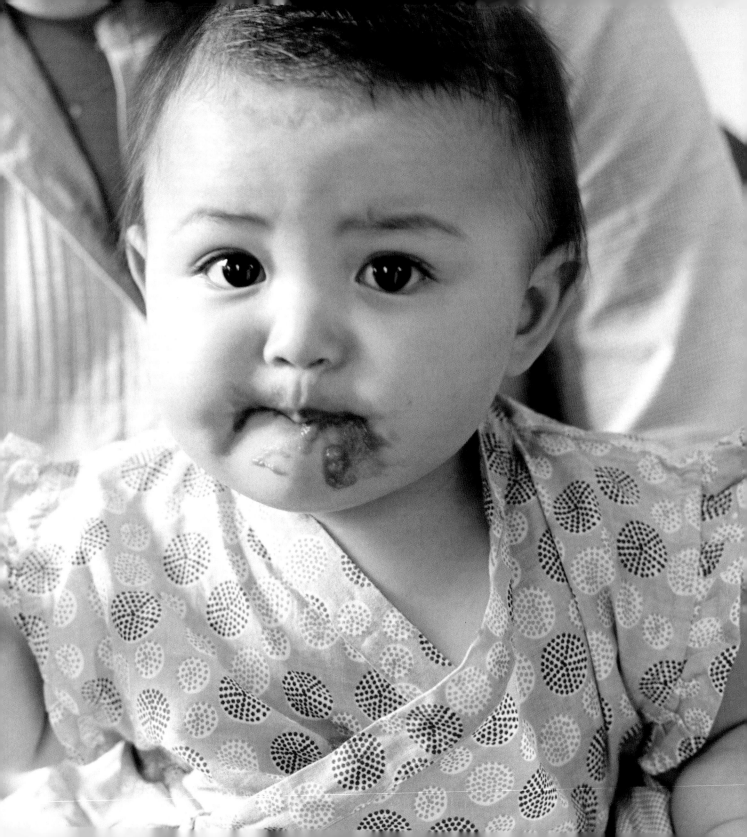

Frances says: At around 6 months your pediatrician will probably say it is time for something a bit more substantial than milk. Heaven to your ears, and to your bleary eyes, for we all trust that a baby with a full tummy is bound to sleep the night. Cereals from the packet are easy, widely available and come with full nutritional information, perhaps all the baby needs. But they don't do much for the taste buds. And good, nutritious first foods are easily homemade.

first real food
purées and spoonfoods

Elisabeth says: First food is something on a spoon, soft enough to be swallowed without chewing – a little taste of what's around, easy to make and won't upset delicate digestions. From mashed peas to stewed apple to rice porridge, every region has a different notion of what this should be. Your baby doesn't yet have a firm notion of what should be on the spoon – as long as it tastes good, that's fine.

1.a

blueberry soup

Scandinavians and Eastern Europeans love a fruit soup as a starter: for grown-ups, chill and top with a spoonful of soured cream and a turn of the pepper mill. Hungary likes its fruit soups made with sour cherries, Romanians prefer apricots, and the Danes favour a mixture of red berries.

Makes about 700ml
Suitable for 6 months
onwards

250g ripe blueberries
500ml spring water
1 level tablespoon cornflour or
ground rice or potato starch

Blueberries, the least acid of the European berry harvest, are the most suitable for babies as they don't need sweetening. They are also high in vitamin C and contain a natural enzyme that allows them to keep for a long time in the fridge.

Put the fruit into a saucepan with the spring water. Bring to the boil, reduce the heat and cook gently until the berries pop and the juices run – 5–10 minutes. Strain, mashing to extract all the juice.

Meanwhile, liquidise the cornflour or ground rice or potato starch by working it with 1 tablespoon water until runny and free of lumps.

Return the juice to the pan and stir in the cornflour. Cook until it thickens – 5–10 minutes (ground rice takes longer than cornflour or potato starch) – stirring throughout. Allow to cool to finger temperature or chill – teething babies find cold food comforting for sore gums.

leek purée

A spoonful of well-cooked leeks mashed with a little potato is traditionally the first food a Belgian baby tastes, even though members of the onion and garlic tribe are not generally considered suitable for babies. Leeks are traditionally valued for the same virtues as garlic: they are anti-fungal, antibiotic and generally good for the health. Even more to the point, they once were the only fresh vegetables available when winter was just about to turn to spring – the right time for humans as well as every other mammal to be born.

Makes about 600ml
Suitable for 6 months
onwards

1 fine fat leek, white part only,
sliced into fine rings
1 medium potato, peeled and diced
spring water

Simmer the vegetables in just enough spring water to cover until very tender – 30–40 minutes. Drain and mash thoroughly, or push through a mouli-legumes (that useful sieving instrument which looks like a drum with a wind-up handle) or blitz in the food-processor with enough of the cooking water to make a spoonable purée.

Clockwise from top left: bluebery soup, leek purée, rice congee

rice congee

Rice is the daily bread of China and the rice-growing regions of South-East Asia, and congee, an unseasoned and unsweetened rice porridge, is eaten much like a slice of toast – for breakfast and as a filler between meals. Light and digestible, it's the perfect baby food. Grown-ups eat it hot; for babies, allow to cool to finger temperature. Indonesian rice expert Sri Owen says her grandmother always made her eat a bowlful of congee when she was under the weather. In Malaysia, baby rice is blended with a taste of salt-cured anchovy – a little extra salt is considered advisable in the tropics, where the body loses salt through the sweat glands.

Makes about 500ml
Suitable for 6 months onwards

100g short-grain rice
(Thai fragrant is perfect)
600ml spring water

All rice, even the rice labelled 'glutinous', is gluten-free, making it non-allergenic. It's also free of extrinsic sugar, the sticky stuff which leads to tooth decay.

If you have time, soak the rice for 2 hours in plenty of cold water, then drain. If not, no matter. Put the rice in a roomy pot and add the water (proportions matter: for a rice to make a porridge, the grains must absorb 4 times their own volume of liquid). Bring to the boil, reduce the heat, lid loosely and simmer gently for at least 30 minutes, stirring occasionally, until you have a soft, soupy porridge. It freezes well – just pop a supply in the ice-cube tray and defrost a portion as needed.

junket

Soft and slithery, the simplest and most digestible of milk foods – Miss Muffet's curds and whey – junket is all about texture. It's the first stage in the cheese-making process, the result of 'turning' (stirring) fresh milk with rennet, a digestive substance found in the stomach lining of all milk-producing animals.

Makes 500ml
Suitable for 6 months onwards

500ml fresh full-cream milk
1 teaspoon rennet (from the
health-food store)
1 tablespoon unprocessed
sugar (optional)

Vegetarian rennet – the substance that transforms milk into curds and whey – is found in a variety of plants, including fig trees, thistles (artichokes, cardoons) and members of the fly-trap family, insect-eating plants which, naturally enough, are equipped with digestive enzymes. Isn't nature wonderful?

Warm the milk to blood temperature, which is the natural heat of the milk when fresh from the cow. Stir in the rennet and sugar and leave to set at room temperature: it'll take a couple of hours to turn to soft curds.

apple purée

Climates which are sometimes chilly – Britain, Scandinavia, North America, New Zealand and southern Australia – are best for apple-growing, and mashed apple is the traditional first food throughout these regions.

Apples are one of a select group of 'superfoods' recommended by nutritionists as particularly helpful for promoting good health: great vitamin C as well as satisfying those early hunger pangs.

Make sure the apples are well scrubbed to get rid of any trace of chemicals to which even organics are not entirely immune: include the skin because even if you sieve it out this means that all the vitamins concentrated near the surface are not lost.

Pack the apple quarters into a small saucepan, add the water, lid tightly and cook for 10 minutes, until the apple flesh is perfectly soft. Mash with a fork and push through a sieve or mouli-legumes, leaving the skin behind.

Makes about 225ml
Suitable for 6 months onwards

4 ripe organic eating apples, washed, quartered and cored
2 tablespoons spring water

pea purée

Peas are the first fresh vegetables of summer, doubly welcome in the cold lands of the north: a soft digestible mash of green peas, the basic ingredient for Denmark's favourite pea soup with dumplings, is the first real food a Danish baby is likely to taste. Danish households have a tradition of careful husbandry and wouldn't want to waste the pods if these were young and tender. If you've bought peas in the pod, drop the empty pods (well-rinsed) on top of the peas to cook in the steam, then scrape out the soft insides to mix with the purée.

Put the peas in a small pan with enough spring water to cover them, bring to the boil, lid tightly and cook for 2 minutes to soften the skins, then remove the pan from the heat. Pop the peas and their cooking water in the liquidiser and give it a whizz. Then sieve – the skins are too hard for a baby's digestion. Or push the peas and their water through a potato-ricer or mouli-legumes.

Makes 225ml
Suitable for 6 months onwards

225g podded fresh or frozen peas
spring water

Peas are an excellent source of vitamin C, B vitamins, protein and fibre. Freezing scarcely alters their nutritional value at all.

sweet potato purée

Sweet potato, also known as yam, can be orange-fleshed or ivory-white, though colour is no particular indication of sweetness. The sweetest is boniato, a white-fleshed variety popular in Cuba.

Sweet potatoes provide tummy-satisfying starch as well as a chill-beating vitamin C. But they're not advised for windy babies, say West Indian cooks.

Orange-fleshed varieties are rich in beta-carotene, the stuff which turns flamingo feathers pink and, if eaten all the time, gives babies a ruddy glow. If your baby seems to have acquired a golden tan, lay off the orange-coloured food.

Makes 500ml
Suitable for 6 months onwards

500g sweet potatoes

Peel the potatoes, chunk into bite-sized pieces and put in a pan with enough boiling water to cover. Return the water to the boil, reduce the heat, lid loosely and cook for 20–30 minutes, until perfectly soft and tender. Drain – not too thoroughly – reserving a little of the cooking water. Mash to a purée with a little of the cooking water.

Clockwise from top left: apple purée, sweet potato purée, pea purée

Frances says: Combinations — foods which together taste good — push the eating experience one stage further. As both you and your baby grow more confident with the bowl and spoon, eating, like all the best things in life, becomes a happy adventure: what *is* that nutty flavour I detect in my squash? You don't know what your kids will like till they try it — and right now they're not capable of being picky.

first real food
bowl food

Elisabeth says: Every region has its own ideas on combinations that work well together and there's no substitute for traditional knowledge at the family level. Balancing flavour and nutritional value comes naturally when you're preparing foodstuffs familiar from your own childhood. Make it easy by introducing new flavours along with the old: mix, matching something you know they like with something they haven't yet tried.

1.b

polenta with yogurt

A cornmeal porridge as they like it in Romania where, as *mamaliga*, it takes the place of bread on the rural table and is always eaten on its own, as a separate course. For children it's combined with something milky – freshly made curd cheese or yogurt or soured cream – adding protein and a touch of sharpness to balance the natural sweetness.

Cornmeal is a suitable grain food for anyone with a wheat intolerance.

Put the cold spring water into a pan and stir in the cornmeal. Bring to the boil, keeping the heat high until the mixture belches and bubbles. Then turn it down and keep stirring as it thickens and ceases to be grainy – 30–40 minutes should see it ready. You can of course make the mixture thicker or thinner as you please just by adding less or more water (if you add water during the cooking, make sure the water's boiling). Remove from the heat and allow to cool to finger heat; it'll firm as it sets. Finish with the yogurt, stirred in or separate, as you please.

Makes about 500ml
Suitable for 9 months
onwards

750ml spring water
150g fine-ground cornmeal
  (polenta)
1–2 tablespoons plain yogurt

quinoa and butternut squash

The nutty flavour and grainy texture of quinoa (pronounced *keen-wa*) is delicious with the sweet juicy flesh of one of the squashes, a combination popular in Peru, home territory of both ingredients. Quinoa was the staple grain food of the Incas of Peru – they called it the mother seed. Modern chemists identify it as being remarkably high in protein – particularly lysine, which is difficult to obtain from any other vegetable source. It also supplies fibre, vitamins B and E, calcium, iron, magnesium and phosphorus.

Put the quinoa grains in a small pan with enough spring water to cover by about 2cm. Bring to the boil, reduce the heat and simmer for 15–20 minutes until the dark skins pop open, showing the pale insides.

Meanwhile, peel the squash with a sharp knife, remove the wool and seeds in the middle (discard the wool, but save the seeds as a nibble – there's a nutty little heart inside) and dice the flesh. Stir the diced pumpkin into the quinoa, bubble up, reduce the heat to a gentle simmer, lid tightly and cook for 20–25 minutes, until the grains are tender and translucent and the pumpkin completely soft.

Makes about 750ml
Suitable for 9 months
onwards

75g quinoa
spring water
500g piece butternut or other
  yellow-fleshed squash

bread and tomato

Every country-bred Italian remembers *papa al pomodoro* as a staple of childhood. Choose perfectly ripe tomatoes and good bread – the kind that weighs heavy in the hand and dries out as it ages – and prepare the dish only when you need it.

Makes about 250ml
Suitable for 9 months
onwards

1 thick slice dried-out
country bread
1 large field-ripened tomato
½ tablespoon mild olive oil

Tuscan bread is unsalted: perfect for babies. Tomatoes are high in antioxidants, rich in vitamins C and E and are classed by nutritionists as 'superfoods' – foods that are particularly good for health.

Tear the bread into little bits. Cut the tomato in half through the equator and, gripping the skin side of one half firmly in your fist, grate the flesh along with the seeds and juices through the large holes of a cheese grater, leaving you with a scraped-out half moon of skin. Repeat with the other half. Push the resulting pulp through a sieve into a bowl. Stir in the torn bread. Add enough boiling water to soften everything to a pulp. Fork over gently and leave for 10 minutes for the bread and juices to mix. Trickle with the oil and fork over again.

red lentils with spinach

The perfect combination of pulses and greens: soft-cooked Indian lentils with fresh spinach, a popular dish at the traditional family meal taken after the work day is over. Hindu households – vegetarian by tradition for religious reasons – are particularly good at combining store-cupboard pulses with leafy greens.

Makes about 450ml
Suitable from 12 months
onwards

50g red or yellow lentils
spring water
100g spinach leaves, picked over
and well rinsed

Lentils are good for vegetarians or anyone on a low-meat diet since they're rich in protein and deliver a good supply of iron and B vitamins. Pulse vegetables, lentils included, are the perfect health food. For babies, cook them a little longer than usual to make them more digestible.

Pick over the lentils, checking for any tiny stones, and put them in a small pan with double their own volume of spring water. Bring to the boil, skim off any foam, reduce the heat, lid loosely and cook for 30–40 minutes, until the lentils have soaked up most of the water and are soupy and soft; add more boiling water if necessary.

Meanwhile cook the spinach in a little spring water – a spoonful should be enough – in a tightly lidded pan for 4–5 minutes, until the leaves wilt. Drain the cooking juice into the lentils and chop the leaves very thoroughly (or purée in a liquidiser). Combine the spinach with the lentils and allow to cool to finger temperature.

Prune compote,
potatoes and carrots,
and chicken soup
with rice

Frances says: Next thing you know, your baby's in a bit of tummy trouble: scarlet-faced with constipation, heaven knows why; or turned bright orange because that's what happens when a person eats nothing but carrot and pumpkin; or broken out in a rash because something didn't agree with the system. Often it's just a matter of making minor adjustments to the diet. Here are some of the first-aid foods which worked for me.

first real food
first aid

Elisabeth says: When my children were growing up in the wilds of Andalusia, our neighbours, subsistence farmers, never consulted a doctor except as a matter of life or death. Camomile tea was taken for a fever, honey applied as a poultice for chicken-pox sores and insect stings. Home remedies, of course, are strictly for minor problems, no more than first aid – though that, if fortune is with you, is often all you need.

1.c

prune compote

Makes about 250ml
Suitable for 9 months onwards

150g ready-to-eat organic
prunes, stoned
spring water

What goes in must come out, preferably without having to try too hard. Prunes work on the digestive system by delivering a natural laxative which stimulates the bowel. They're also a good source of iron in easily assimilable form. For extra soothe-power, stir in a spoonful of yogurt.

Put the prunes in a small pan with enough spring water to submerge them. Bring to the boil, reduce the heat and simmer for about 15 minutes, until the prunes are completely pulpy. Liquidise with the cooking liquid and, for younger babies, sieve.

potatoes and carrots

Makes about 600ml
Suitable for 9 months onwards

about 150g peeled, diced potato
about 150g scraped, diced carrot
spring water

This is the Turkish fixer for a runny tummy – it works by acting as a stomach-liner, which is about all anyone can hope for right now.

Rinse the vegetables and put them in a saucepan with enough cold spring water to cover. Bring to the boil, reduce the heat and simmer for 15–20 minutes, until both vegetables are perfectly tender. Mash them with a little of the cooking water and serve as much as your baby will eat.

chicken soup with rice

Makes about 500ml
Suitable for 9 months
onwards

500g bony chicken bits
(wing-tips, back, neck)
1 large carrot, scraped and chunked
green tops of 1–2 leeks or
1 onion, quartered
1 litre spring water
100g white rice

Whatever the reason – convalescence, sudden discovery of an allergy, loss of appetite – there's always a moment for back-to-basics. Rice cooked in home-made chicken broth – the Mediterranean cure-all – fits the bill. Make it with organically reared, free-range chicken bits.

Rinse the chicken bits and the vegetables and put them in a roomy pot with the spring water. Bring to the boil, allow a single belch and skim off the grey foam that rises. Reduce the heat and simmer gently for 30–40 minutes, until well flavoured and reduced by half. Strain, discarding the solids, blot the surface of the soup with kitchen paper to remove any traces of fat, cool, and store in the fridge for no longer than a week. To keep for longer, freeze in ice-cube trays.

Measure 300ml of the broth into a small pan, add the rice, bring to the boil, stir, reduce the heat and simmer for 30 minutes, till the rice is perfectly soft and tender.

lemon barley water

An old-fashioned home-made recipe familiar in its commercial form. Avoid the E-numbers and make your own.

Popular in rural Britain, particularly in Scotland (where adults take it with honey and a tot of whisky); this version comes from southern Spain, a corner-cupboard remedy from the hills of Andalucia.

Lemon disinfects, sugar comforts and barley broth soothes – just what you need when your baby is feeling under the weather.

Drain the barley and put it in a roomy pan with the lemon zest and spring water. Bring to the boil, reduce the heat, lid loosely and simmer gently for 30–40 minutes, until the barley is soft and the cooking broth is milky and lightly thickened. Strain out the solids and return the broth to the pan.

Stir in the sugar and heat gently, stirring with a wooden spoon until the granules are dissolved. Remove from the heat and stir in the lemon juice.

Dilute to taste – drink it warm in winter and chilled in summer – or adminster it undiluted by the spoonful as a soother for a cough or sore throat. You can bottle it and keep it in the fridge for no longer than a week, or freeze it for emergencies.

Makes about 500ml
Suitable for 9 months onwards

1 tablespoon pearl barley, soaked
   for 2–3 hours or overnight
finely pared zest and juice of
   1 lemon
500ml spring water
2 tablespoons unbleached sugar

garlic broth

This is a general cure-all and stomach-settler for babies and young children throughout the lands of the Mediterranean, though this particular version is from Provence.

The brew is also good for indigestion and general discomfort when you're pregnant. Garlic, say modern chemists, is antibiotic and antifungal – which might explain why it figures in fairytales as a defence against witches and other undesirables, particularly vampires and things that go bump in the night.

Simmer the garlic and oil in the spring water for 30 minutes. Five minutes before the end of the cooking, add the sage: it'll give the soup a delicate amber tinge and a wonderfully medicinal fragrance. Season with a little salt. For older children and convalescents, stir in a handful of vermicelli – they'll only take 2–3 minutes – and whisk in an egg yolk after you take the broth off the heat.

Makes 500ml
Suitable for 9 months onwards

6 garlic cloves, skinned
  and crushed
2 tablespoons olive oil
500ml spring water
1 sprig of sage
½ teaspoon salt

mangu

This is a smooth porridge made with mashed cooked plantain, the remedy for an upset tummy in the Dominican Republic and throughout the Caribbean. Plantain, botanically identical to the banana though it never ripens to full softness and sweetness, is one of the most important starch vegetables of the region. The purpose-bred varieties are inedibly bitter when raw; when cooked, they're starchy and bland, and are grown as a staple food in the tropics where grain does not thrive.

Skin the plantains with a very sharp knife – the skin is very firmly attached to the flesh – chop roughly and cook in boiling water. Alternatively, bake at 230°C/450°F/gas mark 8 for 20–30 minutes till cooked right through, then split down the middle with a sharp knife and scoop out the flesh. Mash thoroughly.

Makes 250ml
Suitable for 9 months onwards

2 ripe plantains or green bananas

All members of the banana and plantain family are high in fibre, vitamins and minerals, particularly potassium.

Frances says: As with most things in kids' lives, parents set the tone. Kids are picky eaters as long as parents let them be. When you say that your toddler won't eat anything except white bread, the reality is that you, the parent, cannot tolerate the storm. But you have more control than you think. Replace the white bread with something good, cut into small bits — not too daunting, not too overwhelming — just so you both know they can do it.

window of opportunity

Elisabeth says: There's an explanation for the window of opportunity. It happens when a baby becomes a toddler, no longer dependent on mother for milk, but not yet able to stray too far. Take advantage while it lasts: once independence is established, every unknown food is likely to be rejected, in case it is poisonous. Practical, really. The more we learn to trust our taste buds when we're young, the more adventurous we'll be as we grow up.

2

patterns

Appeal to your child's sense of wonder by presenting combinations of foods in their unchanged state, as close to natural as possible, which not only taste good together but also look beautiful at first sight.

Encourage appreciation by setting up a pretty tasting-menu – what four-year-old Sophie calls 'patrons' – choosing for looks as well as taste. At this early stage, when a child is tasting almost everything edible it encounters for the first time, it makes sense for everyone to make the best of it. Beautiful presentation isn't cheating: successful restaurateurs do it all the time. A chef's reputation rests on his or her ability to transform perfectly ordinary ingredients into something more appealing than the customer could make at home: a dish people are willing to pay for. Presentation – artistry on a plate – ensures a good appetite, promising that the food will taste as good as it looks.

How you achieve this is up to you. Here are a few of the more obvious choices:

- slices of red-skinned apple stacked with slivers of yellow cheese
- orange segments or dried apricots sandwiched with squares of dark chocolate
- slivers of fresh peach with salty, dry-cured ham – prosciutto or serrano
- slices of plain-cooked new potatoes with scraps of crispy bacon
- tomato with mozzarella

Combinations are whatever suits the season and your purse. Just do it together and have fun.

butterbeans with greens
limeños con espinacas

Butter beans or limas, Chile's native beans, are the largest and most delicate of the haricot tribe. This is a creamy bean soup finished with greens which won't be overwhelmed by the flavour of the plain-cooked beans. Choose a mixture of salad leaves – rocket, watercress, mustard greens, baby spinach, mizuna. Haricots are inclined to produce flatulence, an indicator that they're rather troublesome to digest. To avoid this problem, babies younger than twelve months can be given a little taste of the cooking broth.

150g dried butter beans, soaked for 3–4 hours
600ml spring water
2–3 garlic cloves, unskinned
1 bay leaf
1–2 tablespoons olive oil
a large handful of mixed greens, shredded

Drain the beans and put them in a roomy pot with the water, garlic and bay leaf. Bring to a rolling boil, reduce the heat, lid loosely and bubble gently for at least an hour, until perfectly tender, adding more boiling water if necessary. Don't let the pot come off the boil until the beans are tender; how long they take depends on how long they've been in store – allow 1–1 1/2 hours. Stir in the olive oil, bring back to the boil and bubble for another 3–4 minutes, until the broth thickens a little as it combines with the oil. Offer the greens separately for people to choose which they'd like to stir into the hot broth.

olives, ham, cheese

Small children love salty things, and nothing is saltier than olives, ham and cheese, the staples of the Mediterranean larder. Needing no preparation, such foods are eaten as between-meal snacks as well as providing something good to nibble while waiting for dinner. No Italian meal is complete without its antipasto; French children expect an hors d'oeuvre to be provided at every meal, even in school; while in Spain tapas take the place of a formal first course. These habits are acquired young and learned by example, since the pace of life in the lands of the warm south is traditionally more leisurely than that of busy northerners and families eat together most days – or at least at weekends. At this stage, kids'll try anything as long as they don't have to sit in the high chair and as long as whatever it is looks interesting and can be eaten with the fingers.

Mediterranean parents allow their children to eat moderate amounts of salt-preserved foods, taking care to ensure their charges eat bread with their nibbles, and drink plenty of water to counter the saltiness. Within reason, babies need to replace salt lost to perspiration in centrally heated homes as well as in hot climates.

The difference between getting your salt quota from commercially prepared snack foods and eating traditional nibbles such as olives and artisan cheese is that behind the saltiness are far more complex flavours, opening up the taste buds to a thousand new experiences. There are still hundreds of different regional cheeses made around the shores of the Mediterranean, each as individual as its maker, and just as many varieties of hams and cured sausages; as for olives – well, the infant palate can be given a miniature tour of all the world's flavours without having to leave home. Such foods are also seen as therapeutic. Italian babies are given a pared-down strip of Parmesan rind as a teething ring; Spanish babies get a chewy little strip of serrano ham to soothe sore gums. And the French, aware of their responsibilities as the gourmets of Europe, see an appreciation of cheese as essential equipment for life: it's not too much for a baby to expect a little taste of Roquefort once a week from six months onwards – not, as you might suppose, to encourage the infant internal flora, but *pour le goût*, so that the child gets the taste.

artichokes with oil and lemon
anginares ladolemono

Purpose: to learn to use fingers as a precise eating tool, exploring variations of taste and texture in the same foodstuff
Serves 2 children and 2 adults

4 regular-sized artichokes
sea salt

To serve
1 lemon, quartered
about 250ml olive oil

The presence of cynarin, a chemical compound said to improve liver function, makes artichokes good for grown-ups who drink wine. Liver problems make people bad-tempered – which does no one any good.

Greek children learn how to dismember an artichoke, the first pleasure of Aegean springtime, very early in their life. It helps to know that the artichoke is a thistle, a member of the daisy family, with green petals ringing a spiky heart which has to be removed before you can eat the base. You can eat the stalks as well if you strip off the stringy outside; just pop them in the pot along with the artichokes. Children can manage a whole artichoke by themselves: no matter if they don't eat it all – this is an adventure.

Trim the artichokes down to the base of the stalk and remove the small leaves at the base. Don't worry about the prickly ends, they soften in the cooking. And there's no need to rub the cut surfaces with lemon to avoid discoloration if you're going to cook them straight away.

Pop the trimmed artichokes into a large pot of lightly salted boiling water. Return the water to the boil and cook the artichokes until tender (about 20–30 minutes depending on size). Test for doneness by pulling away one of the outer leaves, which should come free quite easily. Drain the artichokes upside down in a colander so the hot water doesn't stay trapped between the leaves.

When the artichokes have cooled enough to handle comfortably, serve with the lemon quarters and a small jug of olive oil so everyone can make their own little dipping sauce, *ladolemono*, by mixing the oil and lemon juice to their taste. Grown-ups usually like 2 parts oil to 1 part juice. Salt is an optional extra and you can replace the lemon juice with vinegar if you prefer.

Alternatively, whisk the lemon juice and the oil together in a small jug for a ready-made dipping sauce, and provide everyone with an artichoke and a little bowl for the sauce. Set a plate in the middle of the table for the debris.

frittered calamares
calamares a la romana

The cephalopods – squid (*calamar*), cuttlefish, octopus – are all about texture: the flavour is delicate and sweet, the mouth-feel firm and chewy. In this Spanish dish, given a light dusting of flour and dunked in hot oil for no more than 2–3 minutes, they're a bit like French fries.

Rinse the squid in a sieve under cold water, leaving it damp. Dust with flour (no salt – salting toughens the flesh) and shake vigorously over the sink to allow excess flour to drop through the holes.

Meanwhile, heat a depth of about 2cm olive oil in a frying pan until lightly hazed with blue. Test with a cube of bread: if bubbles form round the edge immediately, it's ready to fry – if the bread browns within seconds, the oil's too hot and should be allowed to cool a little.

Separate the squid rings with your fingers and drop them into the oil a few at a time to avoid lowering the temperature. Remove with a draining spoon as soon the flesh turns opaque – don't overcook or it will toughen – and transfer to kitchen paper.

Continue until all are done. Allow to cool a little so no one burns their fingers. A squeeze of lemon will cut the richness.

Purpose: to explore fishy and chewy food
Serves 2 children and 2 adults

500g ready-cleaned squid, sliced into rings
2 tablespoons strong bread flour
light olive oil for shallow-frying

After handling fish, rinse your hands in cold water and they'll never smell fishy. Magic.

asparagus with eggs
asparagi al uovo

Asparagus is easy to handle and fun to eat, particularly with a dipping sauce of hard-boiled egg mashed up with olive oil, which is the way they like it in Udine, in northern Italy, where they grow early asparagus for the markets of Austria and Germany.

Bring the eggs up to room temperature before you begin. Place them in a small pan with enough cold water to submerge them completely. Bring the water to the boil, reduce the heat to a robust simmer, and cook for 6 minutes – no more. Remove the eggs with a draining spoon and hold them under the cold tap for a minute to stop the cooking process and loosen the shells ready for peeling.

Wash and trim the asparagus, removing the dry ends and peeling off any tough skin.

Bring a panful of lightly salted water to the boil in a tall narrow pan which will accommodate the asparagus vertically, or lay the spears in a deep roasting tin, cover with boiling water, add a little salt and bring to the boil. Cook for 6–10 minutes, depending on the thickness of the spears, until the tips are tender but the stalks not yet floppy. Drain carefully and allow to cool to finger temperature.

Serve each person with a few spears of asparagus, a shelled egg for mashing and enough oil to make a dipping sauce. Provide sea salt or not, as you please.

**Purpose: to explore mouth-feel, combining sauce ingredients to suit yourself
Serves 2 children and 2 adults**

500g fresh asparagus spears
sea salt

To serve
4 organic free-range eggs,
   hard-boiled
olive oil

Frances says: You're still not sure exactly how it happened, but somehow your neat little handbag that once held a lipstick and boyfriend's keys is now full of cheerios, crackers or just crumbs. This is the magic stage, the time when a baby will eat anything, so long as you and everyone within eyeshot is eating it too. Eating becomes a social activity and tasting what everyone else is eating means being part of the gang.

join the gang

Elisabeth says: The recipes in this section are family dishes from around the world, real classics, the kind of meals you remember when you're far from home. Most, though not all, are based on a grain food sauced with something soupy. Meat is used sparingly: grain food is the mainstay of everyone's daily diet. Most are prepared in a single pot – cooking implements and heat sources were precious when these recipes were first devised.

3

Scotch broth

A lamb stew thick with vegetables and fortified with barley, a Scotch broth is usually served as the main course of a family meal. The barley provides the basic grain food, taking the place of oatcakes or bread.

Serves 2 children and 2 adults

750g neck of lamb, chunked
100g pearl barley, soaked for
3–4 hours or overnight
1kg potatoes, peeled and chunked
2 large carrots, scraped and diced
2 good-sized leeks,
trimmed and sliced
1–2 bay leaves
salt and pepper
a handful of frozen
peas (optional)

Put the meat into a roomy casserole with the barley and its soaking water, the potatoes, carrots, leeks, bay leaves and salt and pepper. Add enough water to submerge everything completely, bring to the boil, reduce the heat, lid and simmer gently for 1 hour.

Alternatively, cook in the oven at 180°C/350°F/gas mark 4. When the meat is soft enough to eat with a spoon and the potatoes have almost collapsed into the broth (about 25–30 minutes), it's done. Check every now and again and add more water if it looks like drying out.

For added child appeal, finish the pot with a handful of frozen peas, allowing them just long enough to defrost in the hot broth.

winter minestrone

A cold-beating one-pot dish from northern Italy which takes its name from the meal at which it's traditionally eaten – *minestra*, the midday break. You can vary the composition as you please: a sunny summer minestrone might include diced tomato instead of carrot and a handful of shredded courgette blossom to replace the cabbage. If you were preparing this in a Tuscan farmhouse kitchen, you'd drop a slice of garlic-rubbed bread in the bottom of the plate before you ladled in the soup.

Warm the oil in a large soup pot and add the onion, carrots, celery and diced prosciutto. Stir everything over the heat for 3–4 minutes to soften the vegetables, but don't let them brown. Add 1½ litres water, bring to the boil, reduce the heat and simmer for 10 minutes. Add the parsley, bay leaf and potatoes. Simmer for a further 10 minutes. Add the pasta and return the pot to the boil. Allow 10 minutes and stir in the shredded greens. Bubble up for another 5 minutes, until the vegetables and the pasta are both perfectly tender, the broth has almost all been absorbed and the soup is thick enough to hold a wooden spoon upright for a second or two.

Taste and add a little salt – the Tuscans get most of their salt from antipasto, and prefer their bread unsalted. So that people can add their own finishing touches, hand round a jug of olive oil, thick slices of country bread with a cut garlic clove to rub on the crumb, and a chunk of Parmesan with a grater.

For *pasta e fagioli* – pasta with beans – stir in a cupful of pre-cooked white cannellini beans.

Serves 2 children and 2 adults

2 tablespoons extra virgin olive oil
1 large onion, peeled and diced
2–3 mature carrots, scraped and diced
2–3 celery sticks, rinsed and diced
1 tablespoon diced prosciutto
1 tablespoon chopped flat-leaf parsley
1 bay leaf
2 large potatoes, peeled and diced
2 tablespoons short macaroni or any medium-sized pasta
a handful of dark cabbage leaves (cavalo nero or spring greens), shredded
salt

avocado with tortilla crisps and black beans
guacamole con nachos y frijoles

Mexico is where avocados come from and guacamole is the Aztec word for something mashed up. Avocados are a miracle foodstuff: they contain just about everything a person needs to keep body and soul together – particularly when eaten with maize-flour tortillas, the bread of the Aztecs. They're high in protein, rich in fibre and carbohydrates, well endowed with all essential vitamins and minerals and, better still for babies, they're easily digested. High levels of copper and iron in easily assimilable form make them good for anaemia. What more can anyone ask?

Combined with other little things that taste good – shredded chicken, beans, fresh white cheese, a few slivers of fiery green chilli – this dish is an adventure in flavours as well as a complete meal in itself.

If your avocados are hard, wrap them in newspaper and store in a warm place for 3–4 days to ripen. Store ripe avocados wrapped in paper in the salad compartment of the fridge: if you keep them in the fridge in a plastic bag, they'll spoil as soon as they meet the air.

Halve the avocados, remove the stones, scoop out the flesh and mash roughly with a fork – don't purée. Fork in the lime or lemon juice, chopped coriander and salt. You can add the chilli to the mash, or provide it on the side for people to stir in their own to taste.

Cut the tortillas into triangles – known in Mexico as nachos, these are the most convenient for scooping. For a tostada, leave the tortilla whole (makes a great edible plate); for chilaquiles, cut into strips (good for adding to soups); for totopos, cut into squares (good for salting and nibbling). Heat a depth of about 2cm oil and drop in the nachos, a few at a time, wait till they crisp and take a little colour (maize-flour tortillas take longer than wheat-flour), then turn to gild the other side.

Serve the crisp nachos with the guacamole. On the side for people to choose what they want, offer crumbled white cheese, shredded chicken and black beans – nicer heated and mashed in a little oil, a preparation known as *frijoles refritos*, re-fried beans.

Serves 2 children and 2 adults

For the guacamole
2 large, perfectly ripe avocados
juice of 2–3 limes or 1 large lemon
1 tablespoon chopped coriander
½ teaspoon sea salt
1–2 green chillies, deseeded
    and chopped

For the nachos
8 small maize-flour tortillas
    (or 4 large wheat-flour tortillas)
oil for shallow-frying

For the accompaniments
about 200g shredded
    cooked chicken
about 175g fresh, crumbly white
    cheese (Mexican *queso fresco*
    or Greek feta)
500g ready-cooked black beans

poppy-seed dumplings
pirozhki

Like Italian ravioli, Chinese jiaozi, Mexican tamales and no doubt a thousand other variations on the same theme, these bite-sized dumplings from Poland, pirozhki (the diminutive of *pirog*, pie) depend on skill and patience. The dough can be leavened or unleavened and the filling can be anything you please: typical of the Polish kitchen are mushroom cooked with onion, minced pork with buckwheat, and potato with sauerkraut, as well as the soft white cheese beaten with poppy seeds I have given here. The method of cooking can be frying, baking, steaming or boiling.

If you have any dough left over, save it for soup noodles: roll it out thinly, cut into little squares or diamonds and dry on a baking rack in a warm corner of the kitchen.

First make the wrapper dough. Sift the flour and salt into a bowl and make a well in the middle with your fist. Crack in the eggs and add the oil. Mix the wet stuff into the dry – easily done in an electric mixer – and add enough water to make a softish dough. Knead vigorously, massaging it with your knuckles and the flat of your hand, until smooth and no longer sticky. Flour lightly, drop into a plastic bag and set aside to rest for 30 minutes.

Meanwhile mix the filling ingredients together lightly; don't overbeat and crush the delicate little seeds.

Roll out the dough thinly on a well-floured board, and cut out 5cm-diameter rounds. Put 1 teaspoon of filling in the middle of each round, wet the edges and fold them in half, pressing the edges together to enclose the dough. Continue until all the filling is used up.

Bring a large pot of salted water to the boil. Drop in the piroshki a few at a time. Wait until they bob to the surface, let them simmer for 2 minutes, then drain and transfer to a warm bowl. Toss lightly with melted butter as each batch is dropped into the bowl. Finish with more melted butter and an extra sprinkling of poppy seeds.

Serves 2 children and 2 adults

For the wrapper
250g strong bread flour
1 level teaspoon salt
2 organic free-range eggs
1 teaspoon oil
about 2 tablespoons cold water

For the filling
1 organic free-range egg,
forked to blend
175g curd cheese
4 tablespoons poppy seeds
½ teaspoon freshly grated nutmeg
½ teaspoon salt

To finish
2–3 tablespoons melted butter
poppy seeds

fresh egg-noodles with cheese
spëtzle mit käse

This is one of the simplest and quickest of noodle preparations which, when layered and finished, makes a most superior macaroni cheese. Once you understand the basics, all the preparation should take no more than 30 minutes from start to finish. It's the highlight of Sunday dinner in the farmhouses of the Black Forest – with a big dish of sliced cold meats and a choice of salads to start and something substantial in the way of dessert to follow.

In Germany they sell spetzle-makers, instruments that look like large garlic-crushers with uneven holes and produce a similar result to hand scraping. Or you can buy ready-made spetzle in a packet: practical and quick, though not as good and not nearly so much fun.

Sift the flour and salt into a bowl. Fork up the eggs until well blended. In a food-processor or by hand, work the eggs into the flour until you have a soft, runny dough which still manages to hold its shape; you may need a little water or more flour, depending on the size of the eggs. Have ready a small wooden scraping-board with a handle – the wrong side of a butter bat or something similar which can be held in the fist – and a small knife. The alternative is a colander and a wooden spoon to push the mixture through the holes.

Preheat the oven to 180°C/350°F/gas mark 4. Fry the breadcrumbs in the butter until golden and set aside. Bring a large pan of salted water to a rolling boil. Heat up a serving bowl, and set a draining spoon and the cheese ready to hand.

If using a board, spread a couple of spoonfuls of the runny egg paste on to the end of it. Using the full length of the knife blade, flick slivers of the egg paste into the boiling water – only enough to cover the surface of the water. Alternatively, press the noodles in small batches through the large holes of the colander held over the boiling water. The spetzle will puff up and firm in a minute or two. As soon as they're done, scoop them up with a draining spoon, drop them in the serving bowl and sprinkle with a layer of cheese. Carry on layering until the spetzle mix and cheese are all used up. Top with the fried breadcrumbs and bake for 10 minutes to set the layers. It's very rich, so serve sparingly, even though a Black Forester could manage the whole thing. A salad of apple and shredded cabbage will cut the richness.

Serves 2 children and 2 adults

About 400g strong
   bread flour
½ teaspoon salt
4 large organic free-range eggs
2–3 tablespoons fresh
   breadcrumbs
a large knob of butter
300g cheese, grated

macaroni with wild rabbit
maccheroni alla cacciatora

In Italy, pasta – large tubular macaroni shapes of a kind suitable for healthy appetites – is sauced with whatever the hunter brings home. Rabbit, venison, pigeon, partridge, quail and wild boar are all suitable for this traditional recipe. Wild meat, free-range and additive-free by nature, is lean, dense, of uncertain age and comes from creatures that have spent their lives romping around the countryside. It needs long, gentle cooking to tenderise it and bring out the flavour, and a little goes a long way.

Put the rabbit, venison or wild boar meat in a large saucepan with half the diced onion and carrot (reserve the other half), the celery, optional wine, peppercorns and a little salt. Add water to cover everything completely. Bring to the boil, reduce the heat to a simmer, lid and leave to bubble gently for 1–1½ hours, until the meat is tender. You may need to add a little more water if the broth looks like drying out. Transfer everything to a sieve set over a bowl to catch the broth, and pick out the bones from the meat, if using rabbit. Return the meat to the broth, discarding the mushy vegetables – they have already done their best – and tip back into the saucepan.

To finish, heat the olive oil in a small frying pan, add the reserved onion and carrot, the garlic and pancetta or bacon and fry gently until everything takes a little colour and softens – about 5 minutes. Stir the contents of the frying pan into the meat and broth in the saucepan. Bubble up, reduce the heat, add the olives and parsley and simmer gently for a further 20–30 minutes, to marry the flavours.

Meanwhile, cook the pasta in plenty of lightly salted water, or according to the instructions on the packet – 15–20 minutes – until it is tender. Drain it, but not too thoroughly, toss with the sauce, and serve in a warm bowl into which you have trickled a little olive oil.

Serves 2 children and 2 adults

1 rabbit, jointed or 750g venison or wild boar meat, diced
1 large onion, peeled and diced
2 large carrots, scraped and diced
2 celery sticks
1 glass (about 150ml) of white wine (optional but nice)
½ teaspoon black peppercorns
salt

To finish

2–3 tablespoons olive oil
1 garlic clove, skinned and finely chopped
1 tablespoon diced pancetta or lean bacon
1 tablespoon black olives
1 tablespoon chopped parsley

For the pasta

350g large tubular pasta (tubetti, penne, rigatoni, ziti)

pasta with pork
fideu a la catalana

The Catalan national dish is a delicately spiced pork and almond-noodle paella which is made in much the same way as the Valencian rice paella. Sometimes, though not always, it includes seafood.

Heat the oil in a paella pan or large frying pan until a faint blue haze rises. Add the meat and onion, sprinkle with a little salt and fry until both ingredients lose their water and begin to caramelise, but don't let them burn. Turn the heat right down, lid loosely and continue to cook until the meat is firm – a sign that it's cooked right through. Remove the lid and bubble up until the pan-juices are oily rather than damp. Push the meat and onions aside and stir in the pasta. Fry until it browns a little. Add the diced tomatoes and bubble up.

Meanwhile, prepare the flavouring paste. Heat the oil in a small frying pan and fry the almonds until golden. Add the garlic and continue to fry for a further minute until the garlic softens and picks up colour. Add the spices and parsley and toss over the heat for a minute or two until the scents rise. Add the saffron and its soaking water, bubble up, then transfer the contents of the pan to a food-processor and whizz to a paste.

Stir the flavouring paste into the pasta, with 300ml hot water. Stir again, bubble up, reduce the heat and cook gently until the pasta is tender and the surface is beginning to look dry rather than soupy. Add another splash of boiling water if it looks like drying out. The pasta should be tender and juicy rather than soupy.

Serve with lemon quarters for squeezing and crisp lettuce leaves for scooping.

Serves 2 children and 2 adults

2 tablespoons olive oil
about 150g diced lean pork
1 medium onion, peeled and
    finely chopped or slivered
salt
250g short pasta (vermicelli
    or elbow-macaroni)
2 ripe tomatoes, skinned and diced

For the flavouring paste
1 tablespoon olive oil
1 tablespoon blanched almonds,
    roughly chopped
2 garlic cloves, skinned and
    chopped
1 teaspoon pimentón
    (Spanish paprika)
½ teaspoon powdered cinnamon
¼ teaspoon powdered cloves
1 tablespoon chopped parsley
6 saffron strands, soaked in
    1 tablespoon boiling water

To serve
1 lemon, quartered
cos lettuce

rice noodles with coconut milk and prawns

laksa lemak

Serves 2 children and 2 adults

250g rice noodles
4 tablespoons oil (sesame or soya)
100g beansprouts, rinsed and
trimmed of any brown bits
1 teaspoon finely chopped
lemongrass
2 tablespoons dried-shrimp paste
or fish sauce or 2 salted anchovies
2 small onions or shallots,
peeled and finely chopped
1 teaspoon ground turmeric
600ml coconut milk
250g raw prawns
salt

To serve
a few fresh coriander leaves
4 small sprigs of fresh mint
1 lime, quartered
fresh green chillies,
deseeded and sliced, to taste

Rice noodles bathed in a spicy coconut broth topped with prawns is a special Sunday lunch for the Nonya population of Singapore and Malaysia. Nonya are a marriage of migrant Chinese workers and the local women, and the spicings in a laksa reflect the mix.

Rice is the main grain food in South-East Asia, and noodles made with milled rice are eaten in much the same way as pasta in Italy, as an alternative to bread. The main protein source of the region is seafood, particularly prawns which thrive in the rice paddies and mangrove swamps, though lots of different insects and reptiles – including snakes, lizards and ants' eggs – are also eaten.

Soak the rice noodles in a bowl of very hot water for 10 minutes to swell, then drain and toss with 1 tablespoon of the oil. Divide between four serving bowls, top with the beansprouts and set aside.

Drop the rest of the oil, the lemongrass and the shrimp paste, fish sauce or anchovies into a liquidiser, add the onions or shallots and the turmeric and grind to a paste. Fry gently in a roomy pot until the mixture smells fragrant, stirring to prevent burning. Add the coconut milk, bubble up, add the prawns and bubble up again just long enough for the prawns to turn opaque. Taste and add salt. Ladle the coconut milk and prawns into the bowls of noodles and finish each portion with a few leaves of coriander and a mint sprig. Serve with quartered limes for squeezing and chilli sliced for those who like it hot – Malay children quickly acquire a high tolerance for chilli.

saffron rice with lentils and dates
addas pillau

This buttery pilau from Iran, layered with lentils sweetened with raisins and dates, is cheap and delicious. The lentils give the rice a pink tinge and the rice is cooked so as to produce a crisp crust. Serve with pitta for scooping, or any of the Middle Eastern flatbreads.

Serves 2 children and 2 adults

350g long-grain (basmati) rice
sea salt
250g green lentils
2 tablespoons diced fresh dates
1 tablespoon seedless raisins
¼ teaspoon powdered saffron, soaked in 2 tablespoons boiling water
2 tablespoons oil
2 tablespoons melted unsalted butter

Wash the rice thoroughly in a colander until the water runs clear. Transfer the rice to a bowl, cover generously with cold water, sprinkle with a little salt and leave to soak for 3–4 hours. Cook the lentils in enough water to cover them to a depth of 2 fingers, allowing 30–40 minutes, until they're perfectly tender and the water has almost all been absorbed. Stir in the dates and raisins, and set aside.

Meanwhile, drain the rice. Bring a large pan of lightly salted water to the boil and stir in the rice. Return the water to the boil, bubble up for 3 minutes, then tip the rice into a colander and rinse under the hot tap. Remove a ladleful of the rice, put it in a bowl and stir in the soaked saffron with its water.

Rinse the pan, return it to the heat with the oil and 2 tablespoons water. Heat until the water evaporates and the oil is clear. Spread in the saffron-tinted rice and fry for a minute or two to evaporate excess water. Top with half the lentils, spread with another layer of rice, top with the rest of the lentils and finish with another layer of rice, mounding it into a dome shape. Poke three holes right through the rice with the handle of a wooden spoon. Wrap the pan lid in a clean tea-towel and cover the pan tightly. Cook the rice on a high heat for 2–3 minutes to reheat it, then turn the heat right down and cook very gently for 30 minutes – longer if you want. Or layer everything into a casserole and bake in the oven at 170°C/325°F/gas mark 3 for 30–40 minutes, until the rice is perfectly tender.

Remove the pan from the heat and set the base in cold water to loosen the golden crust which you hope has formed on the bottom. Unmould the rest of the rice and lentils on to a warm serving plate and trickle with the melted butter. Carefully unstick the crisp crust and drop it onto the buttery mound – if the pan hasn't managed to produce a crust, no matter – better luck next time.

Lentils have a special place in the food mythology of the Middle East as promoters of happiness and bringers of prosperity. In Egypt, they are considered mind-expanding, heart-warming and therefore good for children: brain food with added cheerfulness.

yellow rice with coconut milk
nasi kuning

In South-East Asia, rice is eaten at every meal in much the same way as bread in wheat-growing areas. When coloured and spiced, it can provide the centrepiece of a family meal. In this Javanese dish, a mound of golden rice cooked in coconut milk is flavoured with cloves, lime leaves and lemongrass and finished with ribbons of plain-cooked omelette.

Soak the rice for 1 hour in enough water to cover.

Drain and transfer to a saucepan with the coconut milk, turmeric, cloves, lime leaves and lemongrass and add a little salt. Bring to the boil, reduce the heat, lid and simmer for 5 minutes, until all the coconut milk has been absorbed.

Turn the heat right down, lid again and cook very gently for a further 10 minutes, until the rice is tender. Wrap the whole pan in a towel and leave for at least 20 minutes for the rice to dry and finish swelling.

Meanwhile, fork the eggs together with a pinch of salt until well blended. Heat the oil in an omelette pan and add the egg, rolling it around the pan so that it forms a flat pancake. Remove it as soon as it sets and cut into narrow ribbons.

Remove the lime leaves and lemongrass from the rice. Mound it on to a flat serving dish – easiest if you first spoon the rice into a basin lined with clingfilm, then invert the whole thing on to the dish. Top the rice with the omelette ribbons and finish with a few lemon basil leaves.

Add sparkle with a couple of Indonesian sambals, little flavouring mixes in which chilli and lime juice are the only certainties. Favourites are sambal tomat (diced tomato, chilli and shallots dressed with lime juice) and sambal terasi (roasted shrimp paste crumbled with chopped chilli, sugar and lime juice). Prawn crackers are the easiest way to provide crunch.

**Serves 2 adults and
2 children**

250g long-grain rice
   (Thai fragrant, for preference)
600ml coconut milk
1 teaspoon ground turmeric
3–4 cloves
1–2 kaffir lime leaves
1 lemongrass stalk, crushed
salt

To finish
2 large organic free-range eggs
1 tablespoon oil
lemon basil leaves

Louisiana jambalaya

Serves 2 children and 2 adults

4–5 tablespoons oil
750g pork ribs, cut into
bite-sized chunks
salt and pepper
2 celery sticks
1 large onion, peeled and
finely chopped
2 garlic cloves, skinned
and finely chopped
1 green pepper, deseeded
and chopped
100g okra, topped and tailed
500g tomatoes, skinned and diced
150g short-grain rice
1 small sprig each of
thyme and sage
600ml chicken stock or water

This is true creole cooking: the name is French and African – *jambon à la 'ya'*, an African word for rice – and usually features the Spanish mix of pork and seafood.

Heat 2 tablespoons of the oil in a heavy frying pan. Fry the ribs, seasoning them as they brown, then remove and set aside. Add the remaining oil to the hot juices in the pan and fry the celery, onion, garlic and green pepper gently until soft – don't let anything burn. Add the okra and fry for a couple of minutes, then add the tomatoes and bubble up again.

Return the ribs to the pan, stir in the rice, add the herbs and stock or water, bubble up, reduce the heat, lid loosely and simmer for about 20 minutes, until the rice is tender: you may need to add a little more water.

Serve with a bottle of Louisiana hot sauce or Tabasco for people to add their own.

chicken with rice and egg
oyako donburi

A satisfying Japanese dish of plain-cooked rice with chicken and eggs, a combination also known as mother-and-child rice.

First cook the rice. In Japan they sell special rice steamers to make it all easy, but the traditional method works well enough. Wash the rice in several changes of water until the water runs clear. Leave to drain in a colander for 30 minutes. Transfer the drained rice to a heavy-based saucepan, add the cold water and bring rapidly to the boil over a high heat. Lid tightly, turn the heat right down, and cook without lifting the lid for 15 minutes. Turn the heat up again (leave the lid in place), wait for 20 seconds, then remove the pan from the stove. Leave to rest, still lidded, for a further 10 minutes.

Meanwhile, cut the chicken into small, neat dice, and set aside. Bring the stock, the soy sauce and the mirin or sherry, if using, to the boil in a medium-sized saucepan. Add the chicken, bring back to the boil and cook for 6–8 minutes, until the chicken is opaque and perfectly firm. Pour in the eggs and add all but a spoonful of the sliced spring onions – don't mix. Return the broth to the boil, then turn the heat right down, cover and leave to cook very gently for 3–4 minutes, until the eggs are set but still soft.

Divide the rice between individual bowls and ladle in the broth, including equal amounts of chicken and egg. Finish each serving with a few scraps of the reserved spring onion, and cover with a lid before serving. Drink the broth from the bowl, slurping as much as you please. In Japan, anyone over three years old is expected to eat with chopsticks. Keep trying: it's not as hard as it looks.

Serves 2 children and 2 adults

500g short-grain rice
750ml cold water
500g boned, skinned chicken
    (breast or leg or both)
500ml chicken stock
6 tablespoons Japanese soy sauce
2 tablespoons mirin or dry sherry
    (optional)
6 medium organic free-range
    eggs, forked to blend
6 spring onions, trimmed and
    finely sliced

chickpea stew with chorizo
cocido con chorizo

A robust Spanish one-pot soup-stew flavoured with paprika, garlic and chorizo finished with potato and spinach. Every region – every housewife – likes a different combination of pulses, vegetables and meat; some versions include a joint or two of chicken and fresh pork or beef.

Drain the chickpeas and put them in a large pan with enough cold water to cover generously. Bring to the boil and skim off the grey foam that rises. Meanwhile singe the garlic cloves by holding them on the tip of a knife in a naked flame until the papery covering blackens and the air is filled with the exquisite scent of roasting garlic.

Drop the garlic and chorizo into the pot and add the pimentón, bay leaves and tomato paste. Bring back to the boil, reduce the heat, lid loosely and cook for 1½–2 hours, until the chickpeas are quite soft. If they're old and hard, they'll take longer. Keep the broth at a rolling boil throughout – don't add salt or let the temperature drop or the chickpeas will never soften. Add *boiling* water as and when necessary.

When the chickpeas are perfectly tender, add the potatoes and bubble up for another 15 minutes. Taste and add salt. Stir in the shredded greens, bring the pot back to the boil and cook for a further 5 minutes or so, until the leaves have wilted and the potatoes are soft. Stir in the olive oil and bubble up to thicken the juices a little.

A cocido can be served as a single course, or as two courses without a change of plates: the broth first (fortified with noodles if appetites are keen), then the meat and vegetables.

Serves 2 children and 2 adults

350g chickpeas, soaked overnight
   in cold water to cover
2–3 garlic cloves, unskinned
100g fresh chorizo sausages
1 tablespoon pimentón
   (Spanish paprika)
1–2 bay leaves
1 tablespoon tomato paste (or
   chunked fresh tomato)

To finish
500g potatoes, peeled and diced
salt
500g spinach or chard, rinsed
   and shredded
2–3 tablespoons olive oil

bread risotto with seafood
açorda de mariscos

A juicy bread risotto – here made with salt-cod, Portugal's national foodstuff – the açorda has affinities with Spain's rural bread soups, ancestors of the modern gazpacho. A family dish, nourishing and fortifying, the recipe makes good use of Portugal's robust country bread. In its simplest form, as a bread-pap, an açorda is the first dish Portuguese babies share with their parents.

To prepare your own salt-cod, choose middle-cut and make sure it's not too white (a sign it's been bleached) and that there's no trace of pink down the backbone (a sign of insufficient curing). Brush off any loose salt, rinse thoroughly and set it to soak in plenty of cold water for 48 hours, changing the water whenever you remember. When the flesh is soft and plump, use your fingers to remove the skin and bones, then flake or tear.

Serves 2 children and 2 adults

350g two-day-old country bread
1 large or 2 medium onions, peeled and finely sliced
100ml olive oil
150g ready-soaked salt-cod, skinned and boned
1kg tomatoes
3–4 garlic cloves, skinned and roughly chopped
¼ teaspoon black peppercorns, crushed
½ teaspoon coriander seeds, crushed
½ teaspoon dried oregano
150g raw prawns or diced monkfish (or both)

To finish
2 tablespoons torn coriander leaves

Tear the bread into bite-sized pieces and set it to soak in a bowl of water for 2 hours. Squeeze it dry with your hands.

Meanwhile, fry the onion gently in half the olive oil until soft and golden – 30 minutes is not too long. Add the soaked cod torn into small pieces. Stew gently for a further 10 minutes.

At the same time, put the tomatoes in a roomy stewpot with the rest of the olive oil, the garlic, peppercorns, coriander seeds and oregano and bring to the boil. Mash with a wooden spoon and cook down to a thick sauce – the tomatoes will need to lose about half their volume.

When the tomatoes are well reduced, push through a sieve, return them to the pan, and stir in the soaked, squeezed-out bread. Add 750ml cold water, bubble up, reduce the heat and simmer for another 20 minutes until you have a soft, well-flavoured bread-pap, the form in which it's perfectly suitable for babies.

Stir the onion and cod into the bread and cook for a further 20 minutes, until the bread is perfectly amalgamated with the broth. Toss to separate the crumbs a little and cook for another moment. Lay the prawns and/or monkfish on top of the crumbs, wait for a few minutes to allow the flesh to turn opaque in the steam, and finish with plenty of freshly torn coriander leaves.

bread pudding with cheese and ham
panada alla parmigiana

Italian households traditionally save leftover bread — crusty and chewy when raised with a sourdough starter and baked in a wood-fired oven — for a golden-crusted savoury bread pudding enriched with eggs and cheese. A fresh tomato sauce adds sparkle: easy to prepare with fresh tomatoes ripe from the field; out of season, tinned or jarred are considered just as good.

This dish is traditionally prepared on a Monday morning with a stock made with the carcass of the Sunday chicken and a flavouring of green celery, onion, bay leaf and a few peppercorns or allspice berries.

Preheat the oven to 180°C/350°F/gas mark 4.

Mix the breadcrumbs with the grated cheese and ham or olives, reserving 1 tablespoon of the cheese for the topping. Beat the eggs with the stock and fold into the breadcrumbs. Tip the mixture into an oiled baking dish, sprinkle with the reserved cheese and trickle a little more oil over the top. Bake for 40–50 minutes, until firm, puffy, brown and bubbling.

Meanwhile, make the tomato sauce. Scald, skin and dice the tomatoes (if using tinned, just cut them into small pieces). Put them into a little pan with the olive oil, garlic and tomato paste, stir, bubble up, reduce the heat, mash with a wooden spoon and leave to simmer down into a thick, jammy sauce – about 20 minutes.

Cut the panada into squares and serve the tomato sauce separately.

Serves 2 children and 2 adults

100g dried-out sourdough
  bread, crumbled
100g parmesan cheese, grated
1 tablespoon diced Parma ham
  or stoned black olives
4 organic free-range eggs
500ml chicken or vegetable stock
1 tablespoon olive oil

For the tomato sauce
500g ripe tomatoes (in winter,
  use tinned plum tomatoes)
2 tablespoons olive oil
1 garlic clove, skinned and
  finely chopped
1 tablespoon tomato paste
  (optional)

beef and carrot hotpot
hutspot

This is one of Holland's traditional Sunday lunches – brown beans with bacon is the alternative. Here, meat and carrots are gently cooked in a closed pot in their own juices, with onion for flavour and potatoes for body.

Slice the meat into fine slivers, and set aside.

Heat 1 tablespoon of the dripping or oil in a heavy saucepan and fry the meat and carrots, stirring so all sides feel the heat, until they brown a little. Season with a little salt and pepper, add half the water, turn up the heat, lid and cook gently without opening the pot. Shake it every now and again to avoid sticking, until the moisture has nearly evaporated and the meat is tender – about 30 minutes – then remove and reserve.

Reheat the pan with the remaining dripping or oil and fry the onions gently for 10–15 minutes, until soft and golden brown. Push the onions aside and add the diced potatoes to the oily juices. Turn up the heat, wait until the potatoes begin to fry, salt them lightly and add the remaining water, then reduce the heat, lid and cook gently until the potatoes are soft – 15–20 minutes.

Combine the meat and carrots with the potatoes and onions and reheat everything in the rich meat gravy.

Serves 2 children and 2 adults

500g lean stewing beef (skirt, for preference)
2 tablespoons beef dripping or oil
1kg carrots, scraped and finely sliced
salt and pepper
500ml water
500g onions, peeled and slivered vertically
1kg potatoes, peeled and diced small

baked aubergine and lamb

papoutsakia

2–3 large firm aubergines, hulled
and halved lengthways
olive oil for frying
2–3 tablespoons grated cheese
(kefalotiri for authenticity)

For the meat sauce
250g minced lean lamb
1 large onion, peeled and
finely chopped
1 tablespoon finely
chopped parsley
1 teaspoon ground cinnamon
1 tablespoon tomato paste
1 glass of red wine

For the tomato sauce
2 tablespoons olive oil
2 garlic cloves, skinned and
crushed or finely chopped
600ml tomato passata or
plum tomatoes, puréed

For the white sauce
50g butter
2 heaped tablespoons plain flour
600ml full-cream milk
1 large organic free-range
egg, forked to blend
¼ teaspoon freshly
grated nutmeg
salt and pepper

A sophisticated moussaka – the Greek shepherd's pie – flavoured with cinnamon and nutmeg, a recipe from the island of Cephalonia. In Cephalonia, as in many of the Greek islands, the Venetians were the occupying power in earlier times, leaving everyone with a taste for the spices the merchants of Venice traded with the East.

Make criss-cross cuts in the aubergine flesh, heat the oil in a roomy pan and gently fry the aubergine halves face down. Cook them until soft (they shrink amazingly) and then transfer to a sieve to drain thoroughly, pressing with a spatula to get rid of excess oil.

Meanwhile, put the ingredients for the meat sauce in a saucepan and let everything bubble gently for 1 hour, until the meat is perfectly tender.

In another pan, simmer the ingredients for the tomato sauce for 30 minutes or so, until thick and rich; it should lose about a third of its volume.

In a third pan, make the white sauce: melt the butter and stir in the flour. As soon as it goes sandy, whisk in the milk gradually and continue whisking over the heat until the sauce thickens. Remove, let it cool to finger temperature, then whisk in the egg. Season with nutmeg, salt and pepper.

Preheat the oven to 180°C/350°F/gas mark 4.

Arrange the aubergines in a shallow earthenware baking dish, cut side up. Cover with the meat sauce, top with tomato sauce and finish with the white sauce. Sprinkle with the grated cheese and bake for about 20 minutes, until brown and bubbling – 30 minutes if you've prepared it ahead and allowed it to cool.

lamb goulash
paprikas

A slow-simmered stew flavoured with onions and paprika, one of the few family dishes that relies heavily on meat. Soured cream is optional in Hungary but essential among Austrians, who picked up the recipe when Hungary was part of their empire.

Purists use pork lard rather than oil for the preliminary frying. In Hungary, these things matter.

Trim the meat and dice it small.

Heat the lard or oil in a heavy flameproof casserole and gently fry the onions and garlic until golden. Push the onions aside and add the meat and turn it in the oniony juices. The whole operation will take 10 minutes and is more like stewing than frying. Add 4 tablespoons water, stir in the paprika and season with salt and pepper. Bubble up again, lid the pot tightly, reduce the heat and stew very gently for 1 hour. Check regularly that the pot has not boiled dry, adding a little water as necessary. When the meat is perfectly tender, turn up the heat and take the lid off the pot. Watch carefully as the juices cook down, and take it off just before anything burns: paprika is high in sugar and its natural sweetness can easily turn to bitterness.

Serve with small pasta cooked until tender in plenty of boiling lightly salted water. Hand the soured cream separately, along with a little dish of hot paprika for people to add as they please.

Serves 2 children and 2 adults

750g boned stewing lamb
(shoulder is good)
2 tablespoons lard or oil
750g onions, peeled and
finely sliced
2 garlic cloves, skinned and
chopped
2 tablespoons mild paprika
salt and pepper

To serve
small pasta shapes (elbow-
macaroni, ditallini or home-made
noodles)
soured cream
hot paprika

Frances says: I am always amazed at how children rebel against food. Why sit at a table when there're forts to build, stories to tell, electric sockets to explore? What I can't beat, I join. Which doesn't mean turning beans into funny-faced caterpillars – I just allow the picky one to make a pattern with what's on the plate, sprinkle on their own cheese, count out their own almonds, take a bowl of crackers into the tent to feed the monsters in the corners.

life's a game

Elisabeth says: Forget the smiley faces on the pizza – mealtime is a chance for a little fantasy. If you're a strictly no-veg person on normal days and you'll only eat pumpkin when you're pretending to be Cinderella or Prince Charming, or if rice doesn't look good to you unless it's cooked in a paella on the beach, or you'll munch your way through a pork chop because that's what firemen do – that's fine.

4

Cinderella's midnight feast
pasta with pumpkin and ricotta

This is what Cinderella's coachman did with the golden coach when it turned back into a pumpkin on the stroke of midnight. Cinderella kindly saved some for the prince.

The prince found the dish so delicious and Cinderella so clever – quite apart from being beautiful and having very small feet – that he asked her to marry him at once. But Cinderella said she'd rather marry the coachman and eat pumpkin pasta every day. Let that be a lesson: if you want to marry Cinderella, learn to cook. The same thing applies if you don't want to marry the coachman – not forgetting he was, after all, a rat.

Serves 4 children

250g peeled pumpkin, diced
2 tablespoons butter
350g farfalle (butterfly pasta)
4 teaspoons ricotta

Cook the diced pumpkin in 4 tablespoons water in a tightly lidded pan for about 10 minutes – the pumpkin should be soft but not mushy – remove and set aside. Reheat the cooking juices, add the butter, and bubble up over a fierce heat until reduced to a spoonful, then remove from the heat and stir in the pumpkin pieces.

At the same time cook the pasta in plenty of boiling salted water according to the instructions on the packet: around 6–8 minutes. Drain – not too thoroughly – and toss with the pumpkin and its buttery juices. Serve the ricotta on the side.

fairy-dust
broccoli with parmesan

Remember what happened when Peter Pan shook Tinkerbell's fairy-dust over Wendy and the boys? They flew to Never-Never Land – and so can you. Broccoli is muscle food, and cheese gives you plenty of energy, so the mixture is just right for chasing pirates or rescuing Indian princesses.

Other vegetables might be carrot sticks, diced squash, new potatoes. It works with plain pasta, too.

Serves 4 children
500g broccoli florets
parmesan for grating

Bring a pan of water to a rolling boil (don't salt – the cheese is quite salty enough), and drop in the broccoli. Return the water to the boil, reduce the heat to a simmer, lid to avoid steaming up the kitchen, and cook for 6–8 minutes until the florets are tender but the stalks are still firm enough to hold.

Transfer to a colander and pass under the cold tap to stop the cooking process and allow the broccoli to remain bright green. Arrange on a plate alongside a shower of freshly grated Parmesan.

fisherman's piece-for-the-pocket
supplì-al-telefono

Use leftover risotto to make little rice balls, *supplì*, deep fried in a breadcrumb jacket. If you're lucky you'll find a scrap of mozzarella buried in the middle that pulls out into long strings – telephone lines – which makes them *supplì-al-telefono*.

You can, if you like, make the rice balls without any filling at all. Or you can complicate things – add a little sophistication – by including a cube of prosciutto and a dab of tomato sauce or ready-made pesto from a jar.

Mix the rice and egg with your hand, and squidge it thoroughly to make a sticky paste. Spread the breadcrumbs on a plate.

Serves 4 children

8 heaped tablespoons leftover risotto

1 large organic free-range egg, lightly forked to blend

about 4 heaped tablespoons dry breadcrumbs

12 small cubes mozzarella

olive oil for cooking

Form the rice mixture into a dozen little balls, dampening your hands so it doesn't stick. Push a hole in each ball with your finger and tuck in a cube of mozzarella. Close up the hole neatly and drop each ball into the breadcrumbs, rolling to coat the outside thoroughly. Leave aside for the coating to set – 10 minutes or overnight.

Preheat the oven to 200C°/400°F/gas mark 6 or heat the oil in a deep-fryer.

To oven-bake, arrange the supplì on a lightly oiled baking tray, brush the tops generously with oil and bake for 20–25 minutes, until crisp and brown. To deep-fry, slip the supplì a few at a time into the hot oil as soon as the surface is lightly hazed with blue; remove when the coating is evenly brown and perfectly crisp and transfer to kitchen paper to drain.

pirate's breakfast
hot-'n'-sour fishcakes

Spicy Indonesian fishcakes flavoured with ginger – what else would a pirate eat for breakfast? You can add a little chilli if you like, but don't blame me if the captain makes you walk the plank.

Serves 2 pirates

250g fish fillets, diced
2 teaspoons ground coriander
1 teaspoon ground cumin
1 teaspoon grated fresh ginger
1 tablespoon grated onion
grated zest and juice of ½ lemon
1 egg white, forked to blend
1 tablespoon chopped coriander
or parsley leaves
4 tablespoons fresh breadcrumbs
salt
2–3 tablespoons oil for frying

Drop the diced fish into a bowl, checking with your fingers for any little bones. Mix the fish with the spices, grated onion and lemon zest and juice, cover and leave to marinate for 30 minutes.

Drop the fish and its marinade in a food-processor with the egg white, and whizz to a paste. Mix in the chopped coriander or parsley and the breadcrumbs, add a little salt and form the mixture into 6–8 little patties – easiest if you have a bowl of warm water to dampen your hands.

Heat a little oil in a wok or frying pan.

Slip in the fishcakes a few at a time, and fry, turning them halfway through, until firm and well browned on both sides, allowing about 2 minutes each side. Transfer to kitchen paper and pat to remove excess oil. Serve with crisp lettuce leaves for wrapping with a handful of rice if you're hungry.

fireman's lunch
grilled pork chops

Every self-respecting New York firefighter goes to work on a chop. Practise your fire drill and eat it on rye with mustard. Caraway improves the digestion, and digestion is important when you're a firefighter in a hurry.

Dust the pork chops on both sides with salt, pepper and a pinch of caraway. Brush on both sides with a little oil.

Preheat a ridged grill pan. As soon as it is good and hot, sear the chops on both sides – wait until the meat blackens in stripes. Reduce the heat, lid and cook for 8–10 minutes, turning once, until the juices no longer run pink. Remove and keep warm.

Drop the rye bread on the hot pan and let it pick up the juices from the meat, crisping the crumb where it hits the metal.

Sandwich each chop, bones and all, between 2 slices of rye – you can spread it with butter and mustard, or not – and eat it carefully, saving the bones for last.

Serves 2 firemen in training

2 pork chops, trimmed
salt and pepper
½ teaspoon caraway seeds
a little oil

To serve
4 slices rye bread, toasted
butter (optional)
mild mustard (optional)

sleepover party
lettuce and bacon soup

Eating lettuce makes you sleepy. Remember when Flopsy, Mopsy, Cottontail and Peter Rabbit went to sleep in Mr McGregor's lettuce patch and nearly found themselves popped into Mrs McGregor's pie?

Shred the lettuce leaves, including the dark outer leaves. Put the diced potato, bacon and spring onion in a saucepan with just enough water to cover. You shouldn't need extra salt – the bacon has enough salt already. Bring to the boil, reduce the heat and simmer for 10–15 minutes, until the potato is perfectly soft. Mash the potato into the cooking broth, add the milk and bring everything back to the boil. Stir in the shredded lettuce, return to the boil and cook for a further 5 minutes, until the lettuce has collapsed into the soup and turned it a beautiful grass green.

Serves 2 sleepy people

1 lettuce, rinsed
1 medium potato, diced small
1 tablespoon diced bacon
1 spring onion, finely chopped
600ml creamy milk

princess-and-the-pea pancakes
apple and cinnamon drop-scones

Everyone knows that princesses are so sensitive they can feel a pea through any number of feather mattresses...which is just as well for the Prince, or how would he know who was the real Princess? Feathery pancakes lightened with apple and flavoured with cinnamon are just the thing for a royal tea party. Cinnamon makes things taste sweeter than they really are – useful when you don't want people to overdose on sugar.

Sift the flour into a bowl with the cinnamon, baking powder and cream of tartar. Fork up the egg with a little of the milk and beat it into the flour mixture with a wooden spoon. Stir in the grated apple and work in enough milk to make a thickish, pourable cream which blankets the back of the spoon. Or drop everything in a blender and process thoroughly; you may need to add a little more flour if the batter is too thin to hold its shape on the griddle.

Set a griddle or heavy frying pan over a moderate heat and rub it with a little butter or oil (a clean scrap of linen is useful). When the surface is lightly smoking, drop on a spoonful of batter – the bigger the spoon, the larger the pancake. After a minute, you'll notice bubbles forming on the surface. When the bubbles pop and form little craters, flip the pancake over to cook the other side.

Pile the pancakes in a clean cloth to keep warm while you finish up all the mixture. Tuck just one pea between the layers.

Makes about 12

100g plain flour
1 level teaspoon
  powdered cinnamon
½ teaspoon baking powder
¼ teaspoon cream of tartar
1 egg
about 150ml milk
½ dessert apple, rinsed and grated,
  including the skin
a little butter or oil for greasing
1 pea

beach party paella

saffron rice with chicken and ham

Serves 3–4 children and
2 adults

2–3 tablespoons olive oil
1–2 garlic cloves, skinned and
finely chopped
50g serrano ham or chorizo, diced
½ small free-range chicken, jointed
into bite-sized pieces
350g round-grain (risotto or
pudding) rice
½ teaspoon (about 6)
saffron threads, soaked in
a little boiling water
salt

Spanish children – and their mums, dads, aunties, uncles and grandparents – head for the beach on Sunday for a paella party. The proper cooking implement is a *paellera*, a broad, shallow cooking pan with handles at either side which sits on the embers of a campfire. A large frying pan set on the barbecue works just as well.

If you're using a barbecue, light the charcoal about 30 minutes before you're ready to cook. If you're cooking over a camp fire and using a paella pan, wait until the fire burns down to a circle of embers before you set the pan on the heat. If you're cooking at the stove, a frying pan will do.

As soon as the pan is good and hot, add 2 tablespoons olive oil and swirl it round to cover the base.

The best way to eat a paella is to sit round the pan in a circle and eat the portion directly in front of you, using a Cos lettuce leaf as a scoop. You won't need a knife or a plate, though a spoon might come in handy for scraping up the delicious crispy bits at the bottom of the pan.

Fry the garlic and ham or chorizo for 1–2 minutes – long enough for the garlic to soften. Add the chicken joints and turn them patiently over the heat until cooked right through – you may need to sprinkle them with a little water to keep the heat low. When the juices no longer run pink, add a little more oil and sprinkle in the rice. Stir for a few minutes, until the grains turn opaque.

Add the saffron and its soaking water and enough fresh water to submerge everything completely – roughly 2 measures of water to each measure of rice. Add a little salt. Bubble up, move the pan further from the heat and cook gently without stirring for 15 minutes, adding more water as the surface dries out. It's ready when the surface is pitted with tiny craters. Remove from the heat, cover with a thick cloth and leave for 10 minutes for the rice to finish swelling.

treehouse picnic
banana bread with cinnamon and pecans

An undemanding recipe and a good one, a tea-bread that is sticky and gooey enough not to need buttering. No one can climb trees with buttery fingers.

Preheat the oven to 180°C/350°F/gas mark 4. Butter a 23 × 15cm loaf tin and line it with buttered greaseproof paper (banana bread is a bit of a sticker).

Sift the flour with the baking powder and the cinnamon. Peel and chunk the bananas and drop them in a food-processor or liquidiser with the honey and eggs. Whizz to a smooth purée. Meanwhile, beat the butter with the sugar until light and white. Fold the banana mixture into the butter and sugar, alternating with the sifted, spiced flour, and turn thoroughly until there are no pockets of dry flour. Stir in the nuts.

Spoon the cake batter into the prepared tin, spreading it well into the corners. Transfer to the oven and bake for 1 hour, until the cake has shrunk from the sides and is well risen and springy in the middle. Check after 40 minutes and cover the top with foil if it looks like burning.

Wait for 10 minutes for the crumb to loosen from the tin before tipping the loaf out on to a wire rack to cool. It's all the better for a few days in a tin.

Makes a 1kg loaf

125g butter, softened, plus extra
  for greasing
250g self-raising flour
1 level teaspoon baking powder
1 teaspoon powdered cinnamon
500g very ripe bananas
  (3 large fruits)
125g runny honey
2 large organic free-range eggs,
  forked to blend
125g unbleached cane sugar
50g shelled pecans or walnuts,
  roughly broken

Frances says: Sniff 'n' seek is a game invented by Sophie's dad when Sophie wouldn't eat up her breakfast. It takes energy and commitment – so what else is new? First comes sniff, which is what happens when Dad inspects the bowlful; and then seek, which follows when the bowl has been wiped clean and everyone has to hide. Dad finds them by following the scent – and the food has been polished off in the name of fun!

sniff 'n' seek

Elisabeth says: Scent and taste together make flavour. Some things are smellier and tastier than others: garlic, cheese, onion, lemon and fish are all scents everyone can easily recognize, even if they've never tried them before. The game provides an opportunity for a little gentle persuasion – new and stronger tastes can be introduced precisely because they're less familiar than the bland foods that may be eaten every day.

5

bean soup with basil
soupe au pistou

A bean soup from Provence, very simple and clean-flavoured, coloured with basil and olive oil. The Provençal pistou is thickened with bread, while Italy's *pisto genovese* has pine nuts.

You can replace the pistou with ready-made pesto if you like, but it won't be as bright and sparky. For a more substantial dish, add a handful each of macaroni and shredded greens. The inhabitants of Nice are particularly fond of chard, *blea* as it's called in the Provençal language, a fondness that has earned them rather a rude nickname which you couldn't possibly guess – could you?

Scents for sniffing: garlic, basil
Serves 2 children and 2 adults

250g dried white haricot or
borlotti beans, soaked overnight
2 green celery sticks,
chopped small
1 small onion or shallot, peeled
and chopped small
3–4 peppercorns, crushed
2–3 cloves
1 large potato, peeled and diced
salt and pepper

For the pistou
2 garlic cloves, skinned and
roughly chopped
4 heaped tablespoons basil leaves
1 thick slice day-old bread
sea salt
150ml olive oil

Drain the beans and rinse them. Put them in a roomy pan with the celery, onion or shallot, peppercorns, cloves and enough water to cover – no salt. Bring to a rolling boil, skim off any grey foam that bubbles up to the top, reduce the heat, lid and simmer gently for 1 hour – add more boiling water if needed – until the beans are soft. Stir in the potato and bubble up for a further 30 minutes, until everything's perfectly tender. Taste, add salt and pepper, and mash the beans a little to thicken the broth.

Make the pistou just before you're ready to serve: drop all the ingredients except the oil in a liquidiser and process to a purée; keeping the blades moving, add the oil slowly in a steady stream, as for a mayonnaise, until thick and shiny.

Ladle the pale, creamy soup into bowls and serve the bright green sauce separately, so everyone can stir in as much or as little as they please.

cheesy potatoes
aligot

Mashed potatoes all stringy with cheese, just as they like them in the Auvergne –
French cheese-making territory – where it's really cold in winter. This dish is
traditionally served at weddings in the spring, when the cows are producing plenty
of creamy milk and the cheese is young and fresh. The perfect cheese is a young
Cantal, still crumbly and sharp; but any other fresh, flaky, white cheese will do.

Boil the potatoes in their jackets in enough salted water to cover – start them in
cold water. When they're perfectly tender – about 20 minutes after the pot reaches
the boil – drain and leave them in the colander until they're just cool enough to
handle. Slip off the skins, return the potatoes to the pan, set over a low heat and
mash them thoroughly, beating to remove any lumps.

Meanwhile, in a small pan, bring the milk and the butter gently to the boil with the
garlic. Beat the hot liquid into the mashed potato. Sprinkle in the cheese and beat
it in with a wooden spoon, lifting the spoon high to incorporate as much air as
possible. As soon as the cheese melts and the mixture is light and fluffy, remove from
the heat. Serve in hot bowls and eat with a spoon.

As a variation, make a dent in the middle of each portion and drop in an egg yolk.
If you stir it in quickly, it'll cook a little in the heat.

Scents for sniffing: cheese,
garlic
Serves 2 children and 2 adults

1kg floury potatoes
salt
150ml hot milk
100g unsalted butter, diced
2 garlic cloves, skinned and
    crushed
250g young, crumbly, white cheese,
    coarsely grated
4 egg yolks (optional)

mussels with oven chips
moules frites

Freshly cooked mussels eaten straight from the shell with a heap of crisp chips – moules frites, the Belgian national snack – are about as good as it gets. No need to flavour the cooking broth with garlic and parsley: fresh seafood needs no help.

Mussels are a natural crop, even when they're farmed. The spat (tiny mussels) swim around until they find a perch – rocks on the tide-line, posts set close to the shore, ropes hanging from rafts moored in clean water in a bay – and settle down to grow, feeding off whatever floats by. Rope-grown and pole-grown mussels have clean shells with a golden-brown tinge and are flatter and narrower in shape than rock-grown mussels, which have thick, battered, blue-black shells and are usually loaded down with a crop of little barnacles.

Drop the mussels into a bowl of water while you make the chips.

Preheat the oven to 200°C/400°F/gas mark 6.

Spread the prepared potatoes in an oiled baking tray, brush with more oil and sprinkle with a little salt. Bake for 30–40 minutes, until the insides are soft and the outsides deliciously crisp and brown.

Meanwhile, scrub the mussels and rinse them well, rejecting any that don't shut when handled, or that are heavy for their size (they're probably full of sand). Use a sharp knife to scrape off the beards – the dark, whiskery tassels that stick out of the shell. Once the mussels have been debearded you need to cook them within the hour – they won't stay alive for long.

As soon as the chips are ready, cook the mussels. Tip them into a roomy pot with a glass of water and a little salt, bring to the boil, lid tightly and let them open in the steam, shaking every now and then; 4–5 minutes should do the trick. When the shells have opened, they're done. At this stage reject any that stay shut. Remove the pan from the heat immediately and serve in bowls. Don't reheat – shellfish toughens if it's overcooked.

Serve the mussels with the chips, warning everyone to be careful not to burn their tongues. A half shell makes a good scoop.

Scent for sniffing: seafood fresh from the sea
Serves 2 children

500g live mussels

For the oven chips
2 large potatoes, peeled and
    cut into fat fingers
2 tablespoons mild olive oil
sea salt

meatballs with cream sauce
köttbullar

Bite-sized meatballs flavoured with nutmeg – a spice from the South Seas with a warm, slightly gingery flavour – are finished in a rose-pink cream sauce in this favourite supper dish from Sweden.

Scent for sniffing: nutmeg
Serves 2 children and
2 adults

500g minced pork or veal (or half and half)
100g fresh breadcrumbs
150ml milk
1 tablespoon finely chopped or grated onion
1 organic free-range egg
½ teaspoon freshly grated nutmeg
salt and pepper

To finish
butter for frying
1 teaspoon flour
150ml soured cream
1 tablespoon tomato paste (optional)

To serve
new potatoes
cranberries

If you're in a hurry, use ready-made pork sausage-meat – empty the meat from the skins if necessary – flavour it with nutmeg, roll it into little balls and dust them with flour ready for frying. Just don't tell the Swedes.

Put all the meatball ingredients in a bowl and knead thoroughly until smooth – have a bowl of warm water beside you for rinsing sticky fingers while you work. Or drop everything in a food-processor and pound to a paste. Shape the mixture into bite-sized balls – the smaller the children, the smaller the balls.

Melt the butter in a roomy pan. As soon as it foams, add the meatballs and cook them gently, turning to brown all sides. Remove as soon as they are completely firm: 6–8 minutes. Sprinkle the flour into the pan, stirring to incorporate the sticky juices, add 4 tablespoons water and bubble up, scraping in all the little brown bits. Stir in the soured cream and the tomato paste, if using, return the meatballs to the pan and bubble up again. That's all.

Serve with new potatoes (the Swedes grow beautiful little almond-shaped potatoes with nutty yellow flesh) and cranberries cooked with a sprinkling of sugar: buy fresh berries, put in a pan with a little water and bubble up until they pop.

chicken rice with lemongrass and lime leaves

khao man kai

Chicken and rice are both delicate enough to accept the flavour of other ingredients. This is a Thai dish to eat with a spoon on a cold winter's night. Lime leaves (whole) and lemongrass (sliced or pounded) both freeze well – just pop them in a plastic bag, store in the freezer and shake out as needed.

Rinse the chicken and remove any fat from inside the cavity.

Settle the bird breast upwards in a boiling pot and pour in enough cold water to submerge it completely. Bring to the boil, skim off any grey foam that rises and add the remaining ingredients. Bring back to the boil, then reduce the heat to a gentle simmer, lid and poach delicately without letting it boil for about 1 hour, adding more hot water if necessary. If you prefer, transfer the pot to the oven once the poaching water has come to the boil, and leave to bubble away quietly at 160°C/325°F/gas mark 3. The chicken is done when the thigh waggles easily in the socket.

Leave to cool in its cooking broth for 30 minutes. Remove the chicken, skin it and strip all the meat from the bones. Meanwhile, bring 1 litre of the broth to the boil and stir in the rice. Bubble up until the rice is soft and the broth has almost all been absorbed, about 20–25 minutes – the dish should be soupy rather than dry. Serve the rice hot with the chicken at room temperature.

Scent for sniffing: lemongrass
Serves 2 children and
2 adults

1 small free-range chicken
1 small onion, peeled and quartered
2–3 celery sticks, rinsed and chopped
1–2 carrots, scraped and diced
1 tablespoon chopped lemongrass (heart only)
2–3 kaffir lime leaves
1 teaspoon sea salt

To finish
250g Thai fragrant rice

garlic chicken
pollo al ajillo

Perfect for sniff'n'seek is this Spanish dish of chicken joints cooked in olive oil with plenty of garlic. Garlic is very mild and sweet when slow-roasted in its jacket. For nibbling, add a choice of little tapas, Spanish-style – useful on a day when you have lots of leftovers in the fridge. Maybe a dish of fried red pepper strips, a handful of baby tomatoes and a few rounds of fresh corn on the cob (drop them in boiling water for a few minutes).

Chop the chicken joints into bite-sized pieces and pop them in a plastic bag with the flour, pimentón and a little salt and pepper.

Heat the olive oil in a heavy frying pan. Add the chicken joints and the garlic cloves, and turn everything in the hot oil until the chicken and the garlic brown a little. Turn the heat right down and sprinkle in the water or white wine. Lid loosely and cook gently on a low heat for 20–30 minutes, until the chicken is cooked through and the juices have almost evaporated, leaving a sticky little sauce of garlicky oil.

So that everyone can have a chance to pick and choose, serve the chicken on one dish and the garlic cloves on another.

Scent for sniffing: garlic
Serves 2 children and
2 adults

1 small free-range chicken, jointed
1–2 heaped tablespoons flour
1 tablespoon pimentón (Spanish paprika)
salt and pepper
4–5 tablespoons olive oil
1 whole garlic head, separated into cloves, unskinned
2 tablespoons water or white wine

lamb korma with cardamom
korma chalau

A mild curry from Afghanistan flavoured with cardamom which is cooked with rice. Afghans take some of their cooking habits from China, some from India and the rest from the Persians.

Cardamom is a small green or black pod about the size of a fingernail filled with oily little seeds. If you heat the seeds gently in a dry pan they smell warm and gingery – which is not surprising as they belong to the ginger family. Some people add them to coffee, or chew them to make their breath smell sweet.

Scents for sniffing: cardamom
Serves 2 children and 2 adults

750g boned shoulder of lamb
4 tablespoons plain yogurt
2 tablespoons unsalted butter
or vegetable oil
1 onion, peeled and finely chopped
6 cardamom pods, lightly crushed
1 teaspoon crushed or powdered
saffron
250g short-grain rice
salt

Cut the lamb into bite-sized cubes. Put it in a bowl, mix in the yogurt and leave to marinate for an hour or so to tenderise the meat.

Heat the clarified butter or oil in a casserole and fry the onion gently for 10 minutes, until soft and golden. Add the cardamom seeds – once the pods are crushed, the seeds can easily be separated from them – and fry for a further minute, until the mixture smells gingery. Stir in the saffron and add the lamb and its yogurty juices. Bubble up, reduce the heat, lid loosely and simmer for 40–60 minutes, until the meat is tender.

Meanwhile, rinse the rice in a sieve until the water runs clear. Put it in a bowl with enough water to cover and leave to soak for 30 minutes, then drain.

Add 600ml water to the lamb in the pot and reheat until boiling. Stir in the rice, bubble up again, salt lightly, reduce the heat and cook gently for 20–30 minutes, until the rice grains are soft and the juices have almost all been absorbed.

Pork braised with cinnamon and onions
hirino stifado

The Greeks like to use cinnamon in a stifado, a winter stew with onions, because the flavour is warm and a little sweet, reminding them of summer sunshine.

Trim the meat, discarding any gristle but leaving the fat – it'll melt during the cooking, tenderising the meat.

Heat the oil in a roomy flameproof casserole and fry the shallots or onions gently, shaking the pan over the heat until they brown a little. Push them to one side or remove and reserve. Add the meat, carrot and celery and fry until the meat takes a little colour. Add the raisins, cinnamon, orange peel, bay leaf and enough water to cover everything completely, returning the whole onions to the pan if you've taken them out.

Season with a little salt and pepper, bubble up, reduce the heat and simmer gently, loosely lidded, for an hour or so, until the meat is perfectly tender and the juices are cooked right down. Add the diced potato and a mug of boiling water, bring the pot back to the boil, reduce the heat again, lid and simmer for a further 12–15 minutes, until the potatoes are tender and their starch has thickened the juices a little. Taste and check the seasoning; if it's a little sweet, sharpen it up with 1 tablespoon red wine vinegar.

Remove the cinnamon stick if you can find it and serve the stifado warm – no Greek likes food piping hot.

As a variation, instead of the potatoes, try including chunks of quince – they have a delicate flowery flavour and a slightly gritty texture rather like a pear.

Scents for sniffing: cinnamon, orange peel, bay
Serves 2 children and 2 adults

500g boned pork, diced
2–3 tablespoons olive oil
500g baby shallots or pickling
  onions, peeled
1 large carrot, scraped and diced
2 celery sticks, rinsed and diced
1 tablespoon raisins
1 short piece cinnamon stick
a curl of orange peel (dried is best)
1 bay leaf
salt and pepper

To finish
500g potatoes, peeled and cut into
  bite-sized pieces
1 tablespoon red wine vinegar
  (optional)

all-pork sausages
bratwurst

German sausages are made with well-minced pork and no rusk or breadcrumbs at all, unlike most sausages – which is why it's worth making your own. You can form the mixture into patties: there's no need to hunt around for sausage-casings, which, these days, are both hard to find and rarely natural.

In Germany, the proper accompaniment is fresh horseradish grated into long, thin strings and mild German mustard which has a delicate, spicy flavour.

Work the meat thoroughly with the seasonings – use your hands and have beside you a bowl of warm water for rinsing. Form the mixture into fat fingers or round patties and dust them with a little flour.

Heat a heavy frying pan or griddle. Fry or grill the sausages or patties – you may need a little oil – until perfectly firm and nicely browned. Check that the juices no longer run pink before you take them off the heat.

Good with plain boiled potatoes and a mushy apple sauce.

Scents for sniffing: allspice, marjoram
Serves 2 children and 2 adults

500g finely minced pork shoulder
1 teaspoon ground allspice
1 teaspoon crumbled dried marjoram
½ teaspoon salt
¼ teaspoon ground white pepper
flour for dusting

old clothes
roupa velha

Greens and potatoes cooked to a crisp crust with salty scraps of wind-dried ham (in Portugal *presunto*) produce a raggedy dish known as *roupa velha*, old clothes. Recipes for potatoes fried with greens pop up under different names – bubble and squeak, hash, scouse – wherever potatoes are grown and people need something cheap and tasty for supper.

Scraps of salt-cod (*bacalhau*, Portugal's favourite ingredient) can replace the meat, or you might like to pop a fried egg on top. Portuguese children like this dish with a few drops of piri-piri, a ferocious chilli sauce from Brazil.

Cook the potatoes in plenty of boiling water until soft – about 20 minutes. Dump the greens on top of the potatoes after they've been on the boil for 15 minutes. Drain both vegetables as soon as the potatoes are soft and the greens are tender but still bright.

If you're using a pan that doesn't have a non-stick surface, heat it first before you add the oil – preliminary heating ensures nothing sticks to the metal. Fry the diced ham or bacon for 1 minute, then add the garlic and cook for 2 minutes – don't let it brown. Add the potatoes and greens and let them fry gently, stirring and turning over the mixture as it browns and crisps. When you have a beautifully crusty heap of greens and potato, push it aside to make a space for the tomatoes. Fry for a further 2 minutes, to soften and brown the tomato skins a little. No need to add salt – there's plenty in the ham.

Scent for sniffing: greens
Serves 2 children and
2 adults

4 large potatoes, peeled
and chunked
2 large handfuls of shredded
greens: Savoy or sweetheart
cabbage, Brussels sprouts, turnip
greens
about 2 tablespoons olive oil
2 tablespoons diced *presunto*
(Portuguese prosciutto) or
lean bacon
2 garlic cloves, skinned and slivered
12 baby tomatoes, halved
or quartered

Frances says: Something strange happens. You call in the babysitter, a friend or granny, and when you come home you are amazed to hear what the kids will eat when Mom and Dad are not around. You are also told that they have been as good as gold and were asleep as soon as their heads went down – and in their own beds. What's going on? Simple. Someone else did the cooking or sent out for a takeaway. If they think it came in a carton, they'll eat it.

the takeaway trick

Elisabeth says: Every parent has a favourite exotic takeaway, something that tasted good at a certain time and that for ever afterwards is a reminder of people and places and fun. For a child, the attraction is the unfamiliar, the element which is not everyday but excitingly somewhere else – like a sunshine holiday in the middle of winter, or climbing on a plane for the very first time, and knowing you're going to a place you've never visited before.

6

ramadan lentil soup
harira

The Ramadan takeaway is a spicy soup eaten immediately after sunset during the month-long fast which devout Muslims observe by eating only during the hours of darkness. When the muezzin calls at nightfall, working people hurry to the nearest marketplace for their plateful of soup – everyone's too hungry to wait. And anyway, the aroma of spices is irresistible. This version comes from Lebanon. The recipe is very variable: some like chickpeas or fava beans instead of lentils, others use different spicings – every region, every town or village has its preference.

Serves 2 children and 2 adults

2 shallots or 4–5 spring onions,
finely chopped
2–3 garlic cloves, skinned and
finely chopped
3–4 tablespoons oil
500g dried green lentils
I short piece cinnamon stick
I teaspoon cumin seeds
½ teaspoon cracked black pepper
I large potato, peeled and diced
salt and pepper

To finish
small bunch of leaf-coriander
2–3 spring onions, finely chopped
finely chopped green chilli

In a roomy soup pot, fry the shallots or spring onions and garlic gently in the oil until soft and golden – don't let them brown. Add the lentils and stir over the heat. Pour in 2 litres of water and add the spices and a little salt. Bring to the boil, reduce the heat and simmer for 10 minutes.

Add the diced potato, bring back to the boil and cook gently for a further 30 minutes, until the lentils are soupy and the potato perfectly soft. Taste and adjust the seasoning.

Finish with a sprinkle of coriander leaves and finely chopped spring onions, with the chilli on the side for people to add what they please.

Japanese noodles with tahini dressing

The cheapest of New York's takeouts, noodles with sesame dressing are a nutritious food fix appreciated by busy mothers and time-pressed office workers alike. The noodles in this recipe are Japanese – either *soba* (the thin, brown, buckwheat variety) or *udon* (thick, brown and made of wheatflour); the tahini dressing is, well, basically Middle Eastern, though sesame – *goma* – is very much part of Japanese cuisine, both as an oil and as a seed.

Bring a large saucepan of water to the boil (no salt). Add the noodles and stir to separate the strands. Bring the water back to the boil and cook uncovered for 5 minutes, stirring regularly. Transfer to a colander, reserving 2 tablespoons of the cooking water. Rinse the noodles through with cold water to stop the cooking process, tip into a bowl and toss with a tablespoon of the sesame oil.

Meanwhile, toast the sesame seeds in the remaining sesame oil in a small pan for 1–2 minutes, stirring until the seeds brown – take care they don't burn.

Bring the reserved cooking water back to the boil and mix it with the soy sauce and the tahini. Toss the noodles in this sauce and finish with the toasted sesame seeds.

Serves 2 children and 2 adults

250g *soba* or *udon* noodles
2 tablespoons sesame oil
1 heaped tablespoon sesame seeds
2 tablespoons soy sauce
2 tablespoons tahini (sesame paste)

Singapore fried noodles
su chow mein

A noodle-based stir-fry with a pinch of curry seasoning, just as they like it in Singapore where the Indian influence is strong. It's quick, too: once all the ingredients are prepared, it'll take no more than 5 minutes from the moment the heat hits the pan.

Chow mein is a leftover dish into which anything goes (within reason), so the recipes are very variable. Chinese egg noodles, Italian vermicelli or thin spaghetti are all a suitable pasta base. Beansprouts, blanched broccoli florets or slivered water chestnuts can replace the carrot, and the spring onion can be substituted by matchsticked leek or slivered garlic. The curry powder can be omitted or replaced with freshly milled pepper or chopped chilli if, like Singapore's children, you like a little heat in your food.

Serves 2 children and 2 adults

250g cellophane (bean-thread)
or rice noodles
2–3 tablespoons light oil
(soya or sunflower)
2 organic free-range eggs
1 large carrot, scraped and
matchsticked
2–3 spring onions, trimmed and
diced into diamonds
2–3 tablespoon shredded leftover
roast pork or diced bacon or
cooked, peeled prawns
1 teaspoon curry powder
about 1 tablespoon light soy sauce

Soak the noodles in boiling water in a bowl for 20 minutes or so, or according to the instructions on the packet. Fork them over every now and again to loosen the threads. Drain and toss with a little oil to stop them sticking together.

Meanwhile, prepare the rest of the ingredients. Fork the eggs together to blend and then heat 1 tablespoon of the oil in a wok or roomy frying pan. Pour in the egg mixture and let it set in a thin pancake. Take it out, roll it up and cut into narrow ribbons; set aside.

Add the remaining oil to the pan and toss in the matchsticked carrot and spring onion. Add the pork, bacon or prawns and turn the vegetables in the hot oil until the carrot softens a little. Sprinkle in the curry powder and stir-fry to blend and develop the flavours. Toss in the noodles and the egg ribbons, turning them to blend thoroughly and allow the noodles to heat, and sprinkle in the soy sauce.

chickpea fritters with sesame sauce
falafel bin tahini

These crisp little fritters are everyone's favourite street food throughout the Middle East – you'll find them in Egypt, the Lebanon, Israel and all points between. Cooked to order and stuffed into a hot pitta-bread pocket with a fistful of salad and a dollop of garlicky hummus, together they make a meal.

You can buy a packet mix for falafel in stores which stock Middle Eastern foods. The Egyptians make theirs with fava beans, the Israelis with chickpeas. In the Lebanon, they like white beans. Each to his own.

Serves 2 children and 2 adults

250g chickpeas, soaked overnight
1 teaspoon ground cumin
½ teaspoon salt
½ teaspoon baking powder
1 tablespoon finely chopped onion
1 tablespoon finely chopped parsley
1 tablespoon finely chopped
leaf-coriander
oil for frying

For the tahini dip
250ml tahini (sesame seed paste)
juice of 1 lemon
1 garlic clove, skinned and
finely chopped
½ teaspoon salt

Drain the chickpeas and dry them very thoroughly in a clean cloth. Drop them in a food-processor and pound to a very smooth paste: they must be very dry and very well crushed or the fritters will fall apart as soon as they hit the hot oil. Add the rest of the ingredients (apart from the oil) in the order given, processing between each addition, until you have a thick paste. Set it aside for 1 hour or so to rest and firm.

Meanwhile, make the tahini dip: mix all the ingredients together until well blended, then taste to see if you need a little more salt or lemon juice.

When you're ready to fry, break off walnut-sized pieces of paste, work each into a small ball and arrange on a lightly oiled plate or place between two sheets of clingfilm. Flatten the balls with the back of a spoon to form little patties.

Heat a deep-fryer or, if using a frying pan, heat enough oil to submerge the patties completely. Wait until a faint blue haze rises and test the temperature with a cube of bread – bubbles should form immediately round the edge and it should brown within 10 seconds. Push the patties, a few at a time, from the plate into the hot oil with a spatula – don't try to pick them up in your fingers. If the oil is too hot, the patties will splutter and split; if it's too cool, the patties will fall to pieces. Should this happen, remove any debris, adjust the temperature and start again.

Fry the patties until the outer shell crisps and browns – the inside will cook in the steam. Transfer the first batch to kitchen paper with a draining spoon, keep warm, and continue until the mixture is all used up.

Serve with pitta bread and chunky lettuce (add cucumber sticks, sliced tomato and onion if you like), with the tahini dip on the side. Eat the falafel as hot as you can bear – they're no good cold.

greens with peanuts
msamba

This is a popular fast food in the street markets of South Africa, where it's made with a variety of edible leaves, including collard greens and the leaves of pumpkin, squash, sweet potato and yam. African cooks like to present clean flavours in simple combinations.

Cook the spinach in a tightly lidded pan in the water that clings to the leaves after washing – sprinkle with salt to encourage the juices to run. As soon as the leaves collapse and soften, remove the lid and add a layer of chopped tomatoes and spring onions. Sprinkle with the powdered peanuts, but do not stir. Reduce the heat, lid loosely and simmer for about 15 minutes, until the tomato flesh has softened in the steam. Stir, lid loosely again and simmer for a further 15 minutes. Remove the lid and bubble up fiercely to concentrate the juices.

Serve with a ladleful of *putu-pap*, the cornmeal porridge of the region. Msamba is also good with grilled corn on the cob – don't add salt, just a squeeze of lime juice to balance the natural sweetness.

Serves 2 children and 2 adults

750g spinach or other greens
½ teaspoon salt
500g tomatoes, finely chopped
6–8 spring onions, finely chopped
4 tablespoons roasted peanuts,
   finely powdered in a food-
   processor

To serve
soft polenta (*putu-pap*)

Dominican kidney beans and rice
habichuelas con arroz

A soupy dish of rice cooked with red beans coloured and flavoured with *sazón*, a tomato and red-pepper seasoning-mix fried in a little oil. Cheap and nutritious, rice-and-beans (a variable dish throughout the Caribbean) is sold by the ladleful in every Hispanic takeaway in New York.

Serves 2 children and 2 adults

250g dried pinto or borlotti or cranberry or red kidney beans, soaked overnight
250g long-grain rice

For the sazón
2 tablespoons oil
2 garlic cloves, skinned and finely chopped
1 medium onion, peeled and finely chopped
½ red pepper, deseeded and finely chopped
1 large tomato, skinned and finely chopped (or 1 tablespoon tomato paste)

The choice of beans varies from island to island: alternatives include black-eyed peas, cow-peas, gingko beans, chickpeas, black beans, navy or haricot beans.

Drain the beans and transfer them to a pan with 3 times their own volume of cold water. Bring them to the boil without salt. Keep them gently bubbling until soft – about 1½ hours. To cook in a pressure cooker, allow 30 minutes.

Put the rice to soak in cold water while you prepare the *sazón*. Heat the oil in a saucepan and gently fry the garlic, onion and red pepper to soften – allow 10 minutes, and don't let them brown. Add the tomato, bubble up and cook for a further 5 minutes, mashing with a wooden spoon, until soft and mushy.

Stir the drained beans into the sauce, add their own volume of boiling water and bubble up. Drain the rice and stir it into the beans. Add about 500ml boiling water, enough to soften the rice and make a little sauce. Lid and simmer gently until most of the liquid has been absorbed and the rice is tender; you may need a little more boiling water. The result should be soupy, spoonable and prettily tinged with pink. Offer salt and pepper so that people can season their own.

Wash it down with a chilled bottle of Sorrel Pop, a refreshing infusion of hibiscus flowers and cinnamon available in any West Indian grocery.

Norwegian fish patties
fiskekaker

Little bite-sized fish patties, cooked in butter and made with nothing but minced fish and cream, are sold as a takeaway from the *fiskemattbutik*, a special minced-fish shop which also sells the same mixture raw – fast food for all the family.

Frozen fish won't do here: it's too watery. Norwegians have instant access to fresh fish – nowhere is more than a few kilometres from the nearest fjord. In ports such as Bergen, schoolchildren, drawn by the delicious scent of hot butter, form queues at lunchtime and take a bagful of *fiskekaker* down to the quayside, swinging their legs over the sea wall and looking out over the ocean as they eat.

Chop the fish flesh roughly, put it in a food-processor with the rest of the ingredients and whizz rapidly to a purée – don't let it overheat or the mixture will separate. Leave for 20 minutes or so in the fridge to firm.

Heat a heavy frying pan or griddle. When it's good and hot, drop in a little knob of butter. When it stops sizzling, drop on tablespoons of the fish mixture, patting each dollop flat with the back of a spoon, and fry, turning once. Don't overcook – allow a maximum of 5 minutes' cooking time for each one. No need to flour the patties – they won't stick.

Serves 2 children and 2 adults

500g filleted white fish (haddock
   is best, cod will do), skinned
6 tablespoons very cold cream
1 tablespoon mashed potato
   or cornflour
½ teaspoon freshly grated nutmeg
½ teaspoon sea salt
butter for frying

Indonesian satay

The satay-seller peddles his wares up and down the streets of South-East Asian cities, advertising his presence by the delicious aroma of roasting spices. On special occasions, you can send for your favourite satay man to set up his little portable box-barbecue in the yard and prepare satay for the whole household.

Anyone with a peanut allergy can replace the peanut butter with mashed chickpeas, or omit it altogether and use 2 teaspoons cornflour for a little extra thickening.

Serves 2 children and 2 adults

500g boneless chicken breast
oil for brushing

For the marinade
1 medium onion, peeled and diced
2 teaspoons chopped fresh ginger
2 tablespoons lemon juice
1 tablespoon palm sugar or honey
2 tablespoons sesame oil
2 tablespoons soy sauce

For the sauce
150ml thick coconut milk
4 tablespoons coarse peanut butter
1 teaspoon cornflour

Skin the chicken breast and cut into neat dice. Drop the marinade ingredients into a liquidiser and process until smooth. Pour over the chicken, turn to coat, then cover and leave to marinate in the fridge for an hour or so. Meanwhile, set 12 bamboo skewers (satay sticks) to soak in water.

Take the marinated chicken out of the fridge ahead of time to allow it to return to room temperature. Remove the chicken cubes from the marinade (reserve the juices) and thread them on the skewers, leaving at least a thumb's width of space at either end.

Make the satay sauce. Scrape the leftover marinade into the liquidiser, add the coconut milk, peanut butter and cornflour (liquidise it in a spoonful of water) and process to blend thoroughly. Tip into a small saucepan, bring to the boil and stir over the heat until the cornflour cooks and thickens the sauce a little. Remove from the heat and allow to cool to room temperature.

Light the barbecue or preheat the grill. Set the satay sticks as close as possible to the heat source and turn them regularly so that the heat reaches all sides. Brush with a little oil throughout. Allow 5–6 minutes, until the meat is firm and lightly blackened at the edges. Serve with the satay sauce.

fried chicken with onions

yassa

The secret of this aromatic Senegalese slow-simmered stew is the deliciously thick bed of onions which provides the cooking juices. You'll find it in fast-food outlets in Harlem, New York, where it's ladled over a steaming mound of rice or couscous.

Yassa is what you make of it, a variable dish in which the only certainty is plenty of onion. The chicken can be replaced with meat or fish (halve the cooking time). Or, for a more substantial dish, include yam dumplings or *foo-foo* – pounded cassava meal. For extra greens, stir in shredded cassava leaves or spinach.

Put the chicken joints in a bowl with the onions, lime juice, salt and pepper and turn with your hands to mix everything thoroughly. Cover with clingfilm and set in a cool place for 3–4 hours – or overnight in the fridge – for the meat to take the flavours.

Remove the chicken joints and pat dry. Reserve the onions and the marinade.

Heat the oil in a heavy enamel casserole or Dutch oven and fry the chicken joints in batches until they brown – 5–6 minutes, turning regularly. Remove and set aside. Use a draining spoon to take the onions out of the marinade and stir them into the hot oil in the pan. Add the carrot, celery and garlic and fry everything gently until soft and lightly browned – 10 minutes or so. Add the reserved marinade and a cup of water and bubble up.

Place the chicken joints on the bed of aromatic vegetables, lid tightly and cook gently either on a low heat or in the oven at 170°C/325°F/gas mark 3 for 40–50 minutes, until the chicken is perfectly cooked and tender.

Serve ladled over rice or couscous, and hand the chilli separately for people to add their own.

Serves 2 children and 2 adults

1kg chicken joints
4 large onions, peeled and
  thinly sliced
150ml lime juice
½ teaspoon salt
¼ teaspoon freshly ground pepper
4 tablespoons olive oil
1 large carrot, scraped and diced
1 celery stick, rinsed and diced
4 garlic cloves, skinned and
  finely chopped

To serve
steamed rice or couscous
fresh red chilli (Scotch bonnet is
  good), deseeded and diced

Frances says: Kids usually get their first taste of unfamiliar cultures when their parents take them to local restaurant. In big cities everywhere, when both parents go out to work all week, most of us don't have time to do everything. Chances are we'll head out on a Saturday evening – at least for a treat – timing ourselves to get there before the rush to be sure of a warm reception.

the restaurant table

Elisabeth says: What you don't always learn in a restaurant are the table manners – the behaviour that fits the food, the pattern of eating you'd expect to find when people of that nationality eat at home. Table manners tell you *how* as well as *what* to eat, something that is not always obvious in restaurants, however authentic the cooking.

So let's pretend...

7

...to eat as they do in France

herb omelette
omelette fines herbes

Serves 1–2

1 large or 2 small organic
free-range eggs
1 tablespoon chopped fresh herbs
(see below)
a knob of unsalted butter about
the size of a hazelnut
sea salt and pepper

French cooks love fresh herbs and use lots of them in cooking and as remedies for minor illnesses. Only the soft-leaf herbs are included in omelettes – parsley, chervil, chives and tarragon are the most important (thyme, rosemary, sage and bay are not suitable). Tarragon is a bit aniseedy and peppery, chervil tastes of liquorice, chives are oniony and parsley tastes carroty and a little sweet.

One large or two small eggs are just enough to make a juicy, soft-centred, child-sized omelette – grown-ups have two or even three eggs. In a French bistro you can always ask for an omelette, even when it's not on the menu, and you can usually choose the flavouring: fresh herbs are particularly delicious, but there is also cheese, ham, mushroom, tomato – or you can just eat it plain. In France, you'd have it with a green salad of curly, bitter-flavoured leaves – frisée or chicory – dressed with a little oil and wine vinegar.

Fork up the egg(s) with a small pinch of salt and a very little freshly ground pepper until lightly blended – don't whisk or overmix. Sprinkle in the herbs.

Set a plate to warm beside the stove. Heat a small omelette pan over a medium heat and add the butter. When it foams, but before it turns brown, tip in the egg mixture. Holding the handle with one hand and a fork or spatula with the other, move the egg as it cooks, drawing the set egg from the base of the pan to form soft, creamy curds. After about 30 seconds, when the curds are just formed but still frothy, stop moving the mixture to allow the base to set. Flip one third of the omelette over on to the middle third, wait for 10 seconds, then roll the omelette out on to a warm plate.

For small children, share the omelette between two. It cuts into strips quite easily and is good with sauté potatoes and a green salad – no tomato or cucumber, just green leaves – dressed with a little olive oil, a drop of wine vinegar and a pinch of sea salt.

table manners

French children join their parents at table as soon as they're able to perch on someone's knee. At traditional family meals, three courses are usual and children follow the same eating pattern as the adults. First comes the hors d'oeuvre, something to nibble while the preparation of the main course is finished: a slice of pâté, slivers of wind-dried ham or *saucisson sec* (French salami) with unsalted butter, sliced tomatoes dressed with oil and garlic, carrots with sesame seeds, shredded celeriac in a mustardy mayonnaise. The *entrée* or main course is eaten with the same utensils (often on the same plate) and might be meat, fish, poultry or eggs.

The cheese course follows, served with a green salad. Then comes fruit – fresh in summer, a compote in winter – maybe with *coeur-à-la-crème* (soured cream dripped through a heart-shaped cheese mould), or a spoonful of *fromage frais*, trickled with honey.

Bread is always on the table for mopping plates, particularly between courses. From a very early age, children are offered a drop of red wine in their water to aid digestion.

...to eat as they do in China

paper-wrapped chicken with steamed broccoli
tse bao gai

Little packages of chicken with fresh ginger and spring onion taste good, lose none of the nutritional value in the juices, look pretty and are fun for children to unwrap. On the side, broccoli for balance, prawn crackers for crunch and plain white rice for bulk. The idea is that dishes that are set on the table at the same time must complement each other and together provide a well-balanced meal.

Put the rice into a roomy saucepan with enough cold water to cover to a depth of 2 fingers. Bring quickly to the boil, turn the heat right down, lid tightly and steam gently for about 20 minutes, shaking the pan every now and again so that the grains are evenly cooked. Or use a rice steamer.

Meanwhile, prepare the chicken breasts. Slice them across the grain into very thin, bite-sized slivers. Mix the soy sauce with the sesame oil and sugar in a small bowl, add the chicken, ginger and spring onions, turn to coat, and leave to marinate for 30 minutes or so. Cut the rice paper or parchment into 12 squares about the length of your hand.

When you're ready to cook, divide the marinated chicken with its ginger and onions into 12 little oblong piles. Lay out the first square ready to receive its filling. Place one pile of chicken diagonally across one corner, leaving a flap. Fold the flap over the filling and continue to fold until you reach the middle of the paper. Fold the two side corners into the middle, enclosing the filling on three sides. Continue folding until

Serves 2 children and 2 adults

200g long-grain white rice
3 chicken breasts, skinned
  and boned
2 tablespoons soy sauce
2 tablespoons sesame oil
1 teaspoon sugar
1 tablespoon finely matchsticked
  fresh ginger
4 spring onions, trimmed and
  sliced
1 packet rice paper or 2–3 sheets
  baking parchment
500g broccoli, cut into
  bite-sized florets
1 tablespoon oil and 2 tablespoons
  oyster sauce (optional)
24 prawn crackers

table manners

Chinese children join their parents at table as babes in arms and are expected to wield their own chopsticks from the age of three. Food is always served in small enough pieces to allow it to be eaten without a knife. All the dishes are set in the middle of the table at the same time, each person has their own bowl of rice and helps themselves from the serving dishes with their own chopsticks, taking only as much as can be eaten in a single mouthful. The division of sweet and savoury is not clearly defined, even when the dishes arrive in a succession of courses, as at a banquet.

Combinations matter: for a meal to satisfy the eater's spiritual as well as physical requirements, the *yin* and *yang* – the feminine and masculine elements of all things – must be kept in harmony. Even everyday meals are carefully composed to provide the correct balance of *fan* (grain food) and *cai* (meats and vegetables). Colour, shape, aroma, flavour and texture are also taken into consideration.

In company, it's polite to serve your guests with the best morsels so they don't need to appear greedy by serving themselves.

you reach the far corner, tucking the flap under to make a firm little envelope. Repeat until you have 12 packets.

Preheat the oven to 230°C/450°F/gas mark 8 and set a baking sheet to heat. The chicken packets must be at room temperature before they go in the oven. Arrange them on the hot baking sheet, brush the tops with oil and put in the oven for 4–6 minutes, until the meat feels firm when you prod the packet. Allow to cool a little before serving.

Meanwhile, cook the broccoli in a steamer; alternatively toss it in a wok in a little oil, adding enough water to cook it in its own steam, and finish with oyster sauce.

Provide each person with their own bowl of rice and serve the broccoli and chicken packages separately. If you are using rice paper you can eat the whole package; with baking parchment, it will need to be unwrapped – almost as much fun. Freshly cooked prawn crackers – just drop them in hot oil and wait until they puff – provide the crunch. You can also put them in the microwave at 100 per cent for 60 seconds, but they won't taste as good.

...to eat as they do in India

chapatis with potato and spinach curry
alu sag kari

Freshly cooked flatbreads – chapatis, rotis, parathas – are the heart of India's family meals, the most important item on the table, serving as wrapper, pusher and mopper for other foods. Rice and dhal provide the bulk – cheap, nourishing and easily increased if more guests arrive at the table. Supporting dishes such as this delicately spiced vegetarian curry are chosen for balance, an important consideration when planning an Indian meal. Combinations – soft with crisp, hot with cool, fortifying with refreshing – are carefully considered.

Preparing a chapati dough is easy with a food-processor – the reward is really fresh breads hot from the griddle. Sift the flour with ½ teaspoon salt into the processor's bowl and, using the dough hook, gradually add enough warm water to make a soft dough – about 500ml. Stop as soon it forms a single lump (1–2 minutes). Tip the dough ball out on to a floured board and finish kneading by hand, working it with your fists until it's silky and smooth. Form into a ball, cover with clingfilm or a damp cloth and set aside for 1–2 hours for the flour to swell (overnight is best of all).

To prepare the curry, heat the butter or oil in a medium-sized saucepan. Add the onion and fry gently until soft and golden – allow at least 10 minutes. Sprinkle with the garam masala and turmeric, add the diced potatoes, stir and add a little salt. Pour in enough water to submerge everything completely. Bubble up, then reduce the heat to a gentle simmer, lid loosely and cook for 20–25 minutes, until the potatoes are perfectly soft and have absorbed most of the golden liquid. Stir in the shredded spinach, turning everything over the heat until the leaves wilt – 3–4 minutes.

Just before the family comes to the table, prepare the chapatis for the griddle. Knead the dough ball until smooth – for a minute or two – and roll it into a thick rope.

**Serves 2 children and
2 adults**

For the chapatis
about 350g chapati flour (roti),
   or 250g stoneground wholemeal
   and 100g plain bread flour
salt

For the curry
2 tablespoons melted butter
   or oil
1 large onion, peeled and
   finely chopped
1 tablespoon garam masala
1 teaspoon ground tumeric
1kg potatoes, peeled and diced
300g spinach, shredded
1 tablespoon cashew nuts
   or almonds, toasted

For the side dishes
plain-cooked dhal
plain-cooked rice (basmati or any
   long-grain rice)
plain yogurt, stirred with grated
   cucumber

Break off a nugget about the size of a walnut, keeping the rest covered under clingfilm, work into a smooth ball, dust lightly with flour and set it aside under clingfilm. Repeat with the rest of the rope. Flatten and roll each ball into a thin pancake (about 20cm diameter) between 2 sheets of clingfilm. Dust lightly on both sides with flour and pile into a bowl under clingfilm.

Place a heavy iron frying pan or griddle over a medium heat. When it's good and hot, wipe the surface with a clean rag dipped in melted butter or oil and drop the first chapati on to it. Wait for 1 minute until little brown blisters appear on the underside. (If the chapati blisters black immediately, the griddle is too hot; if no blisters appear at all, it's too cool.) Turn it and bake the other side for a further minute, pressing the edges with a folded tea-towel to trap the air in the middle and create bubbles. Continue until all are done, piling the cooked chapatis into a clean cloth.

Meanwhile, reheat the curry and finish it by adding the toasted nuts. Set it on the table along with the side dishes, judging amounts according to appetites. Serve the chapatis in a basket, well wrapped to keep them warm and soft. If you cook on gas, the chapatis can be puffed first: hold each one in the gas flame for a few seconds, then turn it to toast the other side, when, magically, it'll puff up like a balloon.

Each person scoops up a little of whatever they fancy with a torn, bite-sized piece of chapati, taking care to eat neatly and not spoil the dish for others.

table manners

Family ties are strong in India. In traditionally organised households, several generations live under one roof and the day's cooking is shared. Side dishes — curries, dhals, rice — are prepared ahead of time by the senior women working together in the company of children; a small baby is always in someone's arms, dozing between feeds. At the end of the working day and after school, everyone gathers at home for the main meal. Children are taught to eat daintily, with the first two fingers and thumb of the right hand only, picking up small pieces of food with a torn-off corner of a scooping-bread, taking great care not to touch another person's portion. Hindu households are traditionally vegetarian: fish is acceptable, but poultry and meat are eaten sparingly — or not at all if the household is strict Brahmin or Jain. Small bowls of the prepared dishes are laid out on the table ahead of time and replenished when empty, while one person stays in the kitchen to roll and cook the flatbreads. Strict Hindus have to throw away any leftovers, so they are careful not to put too much on the table and never take more than they can eat in one mouthful.

...to eat as they do in Scandinavia

Swedish cold table
smorgasbord

A *smorgasbord* without pickled herrings is unthinkable – never mind if you don't like herring, just eat up your gravadlax and thank heaven for new potatoes. The Scandinavian cold table – *smorgasbord*, though only in Sweden – is an arrangement of small dishes, mostly fishy, which can easily be prepared from the store-cupboard, a relaxed way of eating that suits the long summer days when the midnight sun shines and no one ever seems to sleep at all.

Prepare the salmon 2 days ahead. Put the fish skin-side down in a china or heatproof glass gratin dish into which it fits snugly. Dissolve the salt in 600ml boiling water, allow it to cool and pour it over the fish; you need to submerge it completely. Cover the dish with clingfilm and place in the salad compartment of the refrigerator for 2 days.

Drain and dry the fish. Rub it lightly with the oil and sprinkle with the dill, cover again and refrigerate until you're ready to eat.

Cook the potatoes with the dill in plenty of lightly salted water – about 15–20 minutes depending on size. Drain well.

Meanwhile, combine the herrings with the cucumber, soured cream and chives. Slice the salmon finely into thin wedges, angling the knife across the grain.

Serve everything separately, with crispbread and unsalted butter, followed by a dish of fresh berries to eat with soured cream as a dessert.

Serves 2 children and 2 adults

For the brined salmon (no-fuss gravadlax)
500g salmon fillet (tail-piece is fine)
25g sea salt
1 tablespoon oil
1 tablespoon chopped dill

For the herring and cucumber salad
250ml pickled herrings, chopped into bite-sized pieces
250ml diced cucumber
125ml soured cream
1 tablespoon chopped chives

To serve
small new potatoes
dill for flavouring (the flowerhead, if possible)

table manners

In Scandinavia and throughout northern Europe, children take their main meal of the day with their parents and use plate, fork and spoon from an early age. In regions where food was traditionally scarce, people took to the use of plates and table implements early and with enthusiasm, perhaps as a way of imposing order by limiting how much each person ate. In the old days, when rural households might be isolated for long periods by deep snow, the store-cupboard had to be filled during the summer to carry the family through the winter, making everyone aware not only of the season, but also of the need to conserve food in times of plenty against the lean months. The traditional spread provided at gatherings still often includes an element of bring-your-own – each family bringing a dish for sharing – reflecting a very real need, since no one household could afford to empty its larder all at once.

Appetites were also limited by deciding which foods were to be consumed first, of which the cheapest and most plentiful was herring. To this day, pickled-herring dishes are always eaten before anything else.

...to eat as they do in Morocco

Friday couscous with chickpea stew
couscous bin tagine

**Serves 2 children and
2 adults**
(although Middle Easterners
would consider it rude to
count the participants)

250g instant couscous
2–3 tablespoons olive oil
250g baby onions, peeled
I medium aubergine, diced
I large carrot, scraped and diced
I teaspoon cumin seeds
I teaspoon powdered saffron
I short piece cinnamon stick
500g tomatoes, skinned and diced
(tinned are fine)
I tablespoon sliced pitted green
olives
2 tablespoons raisins
250ml cooked chickpeas
(tinned are fine)

To serve (optional)
I tablespoon harissa (Moroccan
chilli paste)

A fragrant heap of little grains served with an aromatic stew cooked in a tagine (the traditional round-bellied earthenware cooking pot), the Friday couscous is Morocco's equivalent of the Sunday roast.

Heat the oil in a well-tempered earthenware tagine or flameproof casserole. Add the onions, aubergine and carrot and stir over the heat until the vegetables brown a little on all sides. Sprinkle with the spices, fry for another moment or two, then add the tomatoes. Bubble up and add the olives, raisins and chickpeas. Pour in enough water to submerge everything, bubble up again, reduce the heat, lid loosely and simmer for 20–30 minutes, until the raisins are plump and the cooking juices are well flavoured and reduced by half.

Meanwhile, set the instant couscous to soak in boiling water according to the instructions on the packet. No need to feel bad about it – instant couscous is as popular with Moroccan housewives as it is elsewhere.

Serve everyone with a helping of couscous and hand the tagine round separately, along with a little bowl of hot sauce made by diluting the harissa paste with a ladleful of the cooking juices.

table manners

Moroccans traditionally eat their food neatly without knife, fork or spoon, using the first two fingers and thumb of the right hand only, which means that hands must be well washed and everything that is set on the table must be soft enough to break apart one-handed. At a traditionally served meal, each person dips into the same serving dish and eats only from the portion in front of them. To pile your food on to your own plate is considered greedy and bad-mannered — unless, of course, you're a foreigner and cannot be expected to know better.

Moroccan children learn from their mothers to roll the couscous into neat little balls by squidging the grains one-handed in the palm. Mothers with toddlers pop the little balls into their children's open mouths, as if they were feeding baby birds. Sweet things are eaten at other times than the conclusion of a meal: Morocco has a vast repertoire of almond and honey pastries, taken mid-morning or mid-afternoon with a glass of iced water, mint tea or sherbet (chilled water sweetened with syrup).

...to eat as they do in Japan

miso soup with beancurd
tofu no suimono

Little cubes of creamy beancurd are dropped into a delicate crystal-clear broth, with no further cooking or additions necessary – well, maybe a few slivers of spring onion or a sprig of watercress. Miso soup is one of the unsung glories of the Japanese store-cupboard: you can buy it as a packet mix, much like a stock cube, or ready diluted in a carton like orange juice. Beancurd (tofu) can be bought fresh from oriental grocers or healthfood shops – rinse, cover with fresh water changed daily, and store in the fridge for no longer than a week. Both miso and tofu are highly nutritious and the combination provides a healthy food fix at any time of day for children as well as grown-ups. It's vegetarian, too.

Heat the miso soup until boiling and ladle it over the diced tofu in individual bowls. Finish each bowlful with a few scraps of spring onion or sprigs of watercress – or not, as you please. That's all.

For nibbling, provide a handful of edamame beans, fresh young soy beans left in the pod and boiled until tender: they're available ready-prepared in oriental markets, where you'll find them fresh in the summer and frozen at other times of year (it's pretty hard to tell the difference).

Serves 2 children and 2 adults

900ml low-salt miso soup
prepared according to the
instructions on the packet
(or see method)
about 350g fresh beancurd (tofu),
drained and diced
1–2 spring onions, sliced diagonally
or a few sprigs of watercress
(optional)

For nibbling (optional)
ready-cooked edamame beans

table manners

Japanese children take their places on the mat with the adults – chairs and table as an eating arrangement are relatively rare – and are expected to treat their food with respect. The Japanese meal is a formal affair, even at home. The main meal is taken between 6 and 7 p.m. and, for the family, usually features three dishes, each cooked by a different method. On important occasions, more dishes are served, though the number is always uneven: party time can feature five, seven, nine. Servings are small and everyone gets their own little portion of individual dishes, served in carefully chosen bowls and eaten with particularly pointy chopsticks.

At its simplest, a meal consists of rice, pickle and a bowl of clear soup. Eating can be a bit noisy: slurping and belching tell everyone how much you're enjoying what you're eating. It's bad manners to talk of important things while eating – best not to talk at all and concentrate on the presentation, a form of storytelling. Dishes are composed to follow a theme mirroring the seasons. In spring, a carrot might be carved in the shape of a blossom; in autumn, a leaf.

Frances says: From a young age, kids want to be included. Stationary babies imprisoned in the high chair love to shake spice jars like rattles; teething babies suck frozen bagels, cold comfort for sore gums. Toddlers bang pots and pans like a set of drums. And once they discover the science of it all, suddenly, faster than you can imagine, they're cracking eggs, measuring cups of flour and peering through the oven door to check the progress of something they've cooked.

cooking together

Elisabeth says: Cooking is and should be enjoyable – there's a sense of achievement in seeing the task through from beginning to end. Start with gathering the various cooking implements ready for use and work through the recipe step by step to the moment when the food is set on the table and tasted. Some of these recipes need no cooking, others require the use of the stove. Unplug the telephone, set the mobile on silent and have fun.

8

crispbread with soured milk and raspberries

flatbrød med saeterømme og rødbaer

Serves 2 children

1 tablespoon soured cream
or crème fraîche
300ml milk
4 tablespoons fresh or frozen
raspberries
1 tablespoon sugar
1 extra-thin rye crispbread

You need 2 breakfast bowls, a spoon and a small mixing bowl (or, if you are in a hurry, a small saucepan, in which case you also need the cooker).

Have you ever wondered how anyone came up with the idea of eating cornflakes with milk for breakfast? Well, it seems that the Norwegians thought of it first. In Norway, where they like to drink soured milk for breakfast, the flakes are made with *flatbrød* – paper-thin crispbreads as big as a bicycle wheel. Combine these with fresh berries in summer and a berry compote in winter. In northern Norway you don't need a freezer to keep your berries frozen in winter – you just store them on the porch.

Stir the soured cream or crème fraîche into the milk, divide it between 2 breakfast bowls, cover with clingfilm and set in a warm place for 2–3 hours – or a cool place overnight (not the fridge, it's too cold) – until the milk thickens a little. To sour fresh milk without soured cream, squeeze in a little lemon juice: you'll still have to wait until it thickens.

Meanwhile, make the raspberry compote. Stir the raspberries with the sugar in a bowl and leave them to make juice for the time it takes to set the milk. If you want to hurry them along, put the raspberries and sugar in a saucepan and heat until the juice bubbles and thickens a little – 2–3 minutes is all it needs.

When you're ready to eat, crumble the crispbread with your fingers over the soured milk – the flakes should sit on top of the milk until you break the surface with a spoon – and finish with a spoonful of raspberry compote.

Dr Bircher's Swiss muesli

Makes about 600g

250g rolled (porridge) oats
100g dried apricots, diced small
50g raisins or dried cranberries
50g sultanas
50g unskinned almonds, chopped
50g unskinned hazelnuts, chopped
50g wheatgerm
1 tablespoon unrefined brown
sugar (optional)

You need a mixing bowl
and a storage jar. There's no
need for the cooker.

Dr Bircher-Benner, a Swiss physician working at a Zurich clinic in the 1920s, invented the famous mixture as a health cure for his patients. It still tastes good and it does you good, and there's no need to buy it in a packet. You can choose other nuts and fruits, but keep the mixture varied for nutritional reasons: every little thing contributes something different.

Mix together all the dry ingredients – the muesli-base – and store in an airtight jar until needed.

To eat, soak in apple juice or milk and wait for 20 minutes until the oats swell – or eat it straight away, as you please. Nice with fresh berries or grated apple.

French hazelnut nutella

Makes about 600ml

150g unbleached cane sugar
75g high-quality unsweetened
cocoa powder
150ml pouring cream
100g ground hazelnuts

You need a small heavy-based
saucepan, a wooden spoon
and 2 sterilized jam jars.
This recipe uses the oven.

I know, I know – no one needs encouragement to eat chocolate and nuts, though nutritionists agree that a peanut butter and jam sandwich is just about the perfect fuel-food. This is a rough-and-ready version of the chocolate-hazelnut spread adored by French children. For added sophistication, use vanilla-flavoured sugar – just bury a whole vanilla pod in the sugar jar and leave it for a week.

Mix the sugar and cocoa in a small heavy-bottomed saucepan. Stir in the cream and bring the mixture gently to the boil over a medium heat, stirring constantly. Reduce the heat and cook for 2 minutes, until the sugar crystals have completely dissolved. Remove from the heat, wait until it cools to finger heat, and stir in the ground hazelnuts, beating until smooth. Pack it into sterilised jam jars and keep it in the fridge for no longer than a week.

Eat the nutella with sour-dough bread and raspberry jam – who needs peanut butter and jam?

Parisian pain au chocolat

The French started it, and now everyone knows what they think this is: a chocolate-stuffed croissant from the bakery, something you'd never dream of making at home. But the real thing is a lot simpler and much more delicious.

What's required is a robust, chewy, just-baked baguette (no fluffy stuff from the supermarket) and the best dark chocolate – grown-up chocolate, not too sweet, with an edge of bitterness.

Push a hole lengthwise through the middle of the baguette with the handle of a wooden spoon. Shove the chocolate into the hole, making sure it's distributed down the full length. That's all.

Serves I

½ freshly baked baguette
50g very good dark chocolate, at least 70% cocoa solids

You need a wooden spoon.

New Orleans granola

This is the American version of Dr Bircher's magic mix (see opposite). It's sweeter and stickier and lumpier and altogether a great deal more delicious, even if it doesn't stick to the ribs in quite the same way.

Preheat the oven to 170°C/325°F/gas mark 3.

Melt the butter with the honey and sugar in a small saucepan set over a low heat, stirring until the sugar crystals have dissolved completely.

Mix all the dry ingredients in a roomy bowl. Stir in the butter-honey mixture, tossing to blend, though not too thoroughly, letting it form sticky little lumps.

Spread the mixture in a roasting tin. Transfer to the oven and bake, stirring occasionally to prevent sticking, for about 25 minutes, until golden – don't wait until it browns: it'll crisp as it cools. The cooking time depends on how dry the ingredients were when you began.

Allow to cool completely before storing in an airtight tin. Eat it by the handful when you're hungry, or settle down with a bowlful topped with milk or cream or yogurt and fresh berries.

Makes about Ikg

2 tablespoons unsalted butter
3 tablespoons runny honey
2 tablespoons unrefined brown sugar
250g rolled (porridge) oats
3 tablespoons shelled unsalted sunflower seeds
3 tablespoons grated fresh or desiccated coconut
3 tablespoons shelled unsalted pumpkin seeds
2 tablespoons pine nuts
2 tablespoons shelled pistachios
4 tablespoons slivered almonds

You need a small saucepan, a wooden spoon, a mixing bowl and a roasting tin. This recipe uses the oven.

Ligurian focaccia
sage and onion pizza-bread

The focaccia is the traditional pizza of northern Italy and is eaten as a snack in much the same way as the southern pizza (an invention, it's believed, of the bakers of Naples). The difference is that it's puffier, thicker and the toppings are simpler: olive oil and sea salt are the basics. Ligurians particularly like sage and onion, with tomato and rosemary as the alternative.

Sift the flour into a warm bowl and mix in the salt and yeast (if you're using fresh yeast, rub it into the flour with your fingertips). Mix the oil with about 450ml warm water in a measuring jug and pour it into a well in the flour.

Using your hand as a hook, work the oily water into the flour gradually till it all sticks together in a soft, sticky lump. Tip the lump on to a pastry board or clean work surface dusted with a little flour, and work it well with your fists till you have a smooth very soft dough ball. Drop it back in the bowl, cover with clingfilm and set in a warm place for about an hour, till the dough is light, spongy and has doubled in size.

Tip the dough back on to the pastry board or work surface and punch and pull it till it's completely collapsed – it'll still feel light and spongy – then work in the torn sage. Cut the dough ball in half and form each half into a ball. Rub the palms of your hands with a little oil and pat each dough ball out till you have a fat, round disc.

Oil the baking sheets and dust them lightly with semolina. Drop a dough round on the middle of each sheet and pat it out to cover the whole surface, pushing it into the corners – it should be about as thick as your thumb. Dust the top lightly with more semolina, cover loosely with clingfilm and leave to rise again for 30 minutes. Meanwhile, preheat the oven to maximum – 230°C/450°F/gas mark 8.

Using the five fingers of one hand, punch the surface of the dough 3 or 4 times to make a pattern of little dimples. Trickle a little oil into the dimples, scatter the top of the dough with coarse salt and sprinkle with warm water from your fingertips. Scatter with the slivers of onion and the olives.

Transfer the baking sheets to the oven and bake for 20–25 minutes until the bread is puffed and golden. As soon as you take the bread out of the oven, trickle it with a little more oil. Cut into squares and eat your focaccia as hot as you can bear.

Neapolitan calzone

A basic bread dough can't go wrong, once you understand the principles. If you have a gang of boys to keep out of trouble, calzone – slipper-breads, pizzas that have been flipped over to enclose the filling – fit the bill.

Sift the flour into a large bowl and put the bowl into a low oven for the flour to warm.

Warm a coffee mug by filling it with hot water. Tip out the water and put in the yeast and sugar. Cream the two together (marvellous how the yeast liquidises with the sugar). Fill up the mug with warm (not hot) water.

Make a well in the middle of the warm flour. Measure in the oil and sprinkle in the salt. Pour in the yeast mixture. Stir it round and add enough warm water to make a soft dough – about 300ml. Knead thoroughly, working it well with your fists (very therapeutic). When the dough is smooth and no longer sticky, put the empty mixing bowl back into the low oven to warm it up again. Remove, settle the dough-ball in the warm bowl and put the whole thing into a plastic bag. Tie the bag loosely and leave the dough to rise for 40–60 minutes, until puffy and doubled in size.

Preheat the oven to 230°C/450°F/gas mark 8.

Knead the dough to distribute the air – it'll lose most of its volume – quarter it, then cut each quarter in 2, giving you 8 pieces of dough. Knead each piece into a ball and flatten it into a thin disc on a floured board with a rolling pin, or sandwich between 2 sheets of clingfilm and use your hand.

Drop a teaspoon of diced ham and cheese in the middle of each disk, wet the edge with a damp finger and fold one side over the other to enclose the filling. Press the edges together. Continue until all the dough is used up and you have 8 little slipper-shaped pockets.

Arrange the calzone on a lightly oiled baking sheet, transfer to the oven and bake for 15–20 minutes, until puffed and golden. If you have a deep-fryer (standard equipment in Italian kitchens) you can fry them like doughnuts.

Makes 8 fist-sized calzone

450g strong white bread flour
25g fresh or 15g dried yeast
  (or follow the instructions
  on the packet)
½ teaspoon sugar
2 tablespoons olive oil
½ teaspoon salt

For the filling
2 tablespoons diced cooked ham
2 tablespoons diced mozzarella
  cheese

You need a large mixing bowl and sieve, a mug and spoon, a plastic bag, wooden board and rolling pin (or 2 sheets of clingfilm) and a baking sheet. This recipe uses the oven.

rags-and-tatters
cenci

Serves 2 children and
2 adults

For the pasta
300g pasta flour
(00 – double-zero)
½ teaspoon salt
3 organic free-range eggs
a little olive oil
semolina for dusting

To finish
a knob of butter
toasted hazelnuts, crushed
honey
yogurt

You need a large and a small
mixing bowl, a fork, clingfilm, a
rolling pin, a saucepan, a draining
spoon, a serving bowl and a frying
pan. This recipe uses the cooker.

This is pasta in its easiest form: a simple, nutritious dough made by kneading flour with egg – nothing added, nothing taken away. And there's no need to mess about with cutting and shaping the pasta: raggedy bits taste interesting and look delicious *because* they're uneven. Children in pasta-making regions such as northern Italy and eastern Europe have it as a treat with nuts, honey and cream – though you can, of course, finish your pasta any way you like.

Sift the flour with the salt into a roomy bowl and use your fist to make a dip in the middle. Crack the eggs into a small bowl, mix them together with a fork, and then drop them into the dip in the flour. Using your hands, work the eggs into the flour, adding just enough water to make a soft dough; if you save an eggshell as a measure, that'll give you about a tablespoonful, which is all you need. Keep pushing and pulling the dough until it's smooth and silky. Form it into a ball and rub it with a little oil. Pop the oily ball into a plastic bag and leave it to rest for 20 minutes.

Dust a board with semolina. Drop the dough on to the board and divide it into 4 pieces. Work each piece into a ball, flatten it with your palm and place it between 2 sheets of clingfilm. Using a rolling pin, roll out each ball as thinly as you can. Remove the clingfilm and cut the dough into small raggedy shapes, rags-and-tatters, with a little pasta-cutting wheel or a blunt-edged knife. Toss the scraps with a very little semolina and drop them into piles on the board, keeping your fingers light and airy so that the scraps don't stick to each other. Repeat with the other 3 balls. Leave the scraps to rest for a further 10 minutes.

Now set aside a handful of the pasta scraps to fry as a crisp topping. Drop a knob of butter into a serving bowl and set it to warm ready for the cooked pasta. Bring a large pan of water to the boil – pasta needs lots of room. Drop in the rags-and-tatters a few at a time so that the water never stops bubbling. Give the pot a quick stir to separate the pasta scraps and cook until

they bob to the surface – 2–3 minutes, depending on their thickness. Remove them with a draining spoon and toss them in the butter in the warm serving bowl.

Meanwhile, fry the reserved pasta scraps in a little oil until they're crisp and puffy. Toss the pasta with the crushed toasted hazelnuts and top with the crispy pasta, a trickle of honey and a spoonful of yogurt.

fattoush
Middle Eastern bread salad

A lemony Mediterranean bread salad flavoured with lots of fresh herbs – easy and great fun to make. The dressing includes sumac, a particularly Middle Eastern flavouring made from dried berries which have a deliciously sharp, lemony flavour.

Split the pitta breads down the middle – not necessary if you're using bread – and toast them. Tear them into bite-sized pieces and drop into a salad bowl. Sprinkle with the sumac or lemon zest and the olive oil, and mix together delicately with your hands.

Now prepare the herbs: pick them over and remove any dirt with your fingers, rinsing them only if it's really necessary and drying them carefully. Strip the leaves from the tougher stalks.

When you're ready to eat, toss the rest of the ingredients with the bread in the bowl, adding the tomatoes, cucumbers and onions first and the herbs last. Dress with about 2 tablespoons lemon juice and a little sea salt.

Serves 2 children and 2 adults

4 small pitta breads or 4 thick slices day-old country bread
1 tablespoon sumac (or finely grated lemon zest)
4 tablespoons olive oil
2 handfuls of flat-leaf parsley
1 handful of purslane (or chervil or extra parsley)
½ handful of mint
6 small, ripe tomatoes, quartered
1–2 small cucumber(s), diced
2–3 spring onions, trimmed and chopped
juice of 1–2 lemon(s)
sea salt

You need a knife, a salad bowl and a toaster.

spinach and cheese parcels
boreki

Crisp little triangular packets of filo pastry, fiddly to make but very good if the filling is as delicious as it should be. Spinach and curd cheese are one of the two classic combinations popular in Turkey, the other being minced meat cooked with onion and spices.

Cut the pastry into strips as wide as your hand – don't unroll it first; you need the full length of the pastry – and keep it covered with clingfilm while you work so it doesn't dry out.

To make the filling, mash the spinach, cheeses and cinnamon together to make a soft paste, seasoning with pepper and a little salt (not too much as the cheeses are already salty).

Put a teaspoon of the filling on the short edge of the first strip. Fold the strip diagonally over the filling to make a triangle, then fold it again to make another triangle – just remember you need to place the cut edge against the cut edge on the opposite side. Continue until you've used up the whole strip and you have a neat little package. Seal the last fold with a drop of water from a wet finger and transfer to a baking sheet brushed with melted butter or oil. Repeat until all are done, leaving a little space between each or they'll stick to one another. Never mind if they look a bit messy, just as long the filling is well wrapped. You can vary the shape by rolling the packages up like little cigars – don't forget to tuck the sides in halfway through to enclose the filling.

To bake, preheat the oven to 180°C/350°F/gas mark 4. Brush the tops of the boreki with melted butter and bake for 10 minutes, until well puffed and golden. Alternatively, to fry, heat enough oil in a frying pan to submerge the boreki. When the oil is lightly hazed with blue, fry them a few at a time, turning once, until the pastry is crisp and brown, and transfer to kitchen paper to drain. Leave to cool a little before eating.

Makes about 24

1 packet (about 250g) filo pastry
250g cooked, well-drained spinach, squeezed dry
100g soft white curd cheese (labna or ricotta)
50g hard cheese (Cheddar or Gruyère), grated
1 teaspoon powdered cinnamon
salt and pepper

To finish
2 tablespoons melted butter for brushing or oil for shallow-frying

You need a knife, a mixing bowl, a fork, clingfilm, a teaspoon and a pastry brush and either a baking sheet or a frying pan. This recipe uses the oven or the top of the stove.

pull-aparts

Bread rolls baked close together so the sides are soft and white when you pull one from the other are perfect for sharing with friends because you don't tear them apart until you want to eat them.

Makes about 18

500g strong white bread flour (unbleached)
½ teaspoon salt
15g fresh yeast or 1 teaspoon dried yeast (or follow the measurements on the packet)
50g butter
about 300ml warm milk
1 egg, forked to blend

Before you begin, set everything out on the table including the mixing bowl and let it warm in the heat of the kitchen. Sift the flour and salt into the mixing bowl. If using fresh yeast, mix it with a little warm water and a pinch of sugar to start it working quickly. If using dried or instant yeast, mix it straight into the flour, or follow the instructions on the packet. Chop the butter into little pieces and drop it into the warm milk, which should be just hot enough to melt the butter.

Use your fist to make a well in the middle of the flour. Pour in the bubbly yeast mixture, if using fresh yeast, and the egg. Stirring with your hand, work in enough of the warm, buttery milk to make a soft, sticky dough. Tip it out on to a clean work surface or wooden board dusted with a little flour (don't bother to clean your hands: the stickiness will come off as you work). Knead the dough with your fists, pushing and pulling until it forms itself into a smooth ball and your hands are no longer sticky.

Drop the dough ball back into the bowl and pop the whole thing into a plastic bag. Tie the bag loosely and put it in a warm place for 1 hour for the yeast to work and the dough to become light and puffy; it's ready when it keeps the mark of your finger when you prod it. Knead it again to knock the bubbles out, and work the dough into a rope. Chop the rope into 18 little pieces. Drop each piece one by one into your cupped hand and form it gently into a neat, smooth ball. Arrange the dough balls in a buttered roasting tin or on a baking sheet with a deep lip, setting them about a finger's width apart. Cover with the plastic bag again and leave to rise for a further 40 minutes.

Preheat the oven to 210°C/425°F/gas mark 7.

Bake the rolls for 30–35 minutes, until well risen and golden brown.

You need a mixing bowl and sieve, a cup and spoon, a plastic bag and a roasting tin or a baking sheet with a deep lip. This recipe uses the oven.

blueberry corn-muffins

Sunny golden muffins to bake for a Sunday breakfast party – never mind if they look a bit lop-sided, they'll still taste delicious.

Preheat the oven to 200°C/400°F/gas mark 6 and warm the milk and butter in a small pan until the butter melts.

Meanwhile, butter a 12-hole muffin tin – the holes are deeper than the ones used for fairy cakes or tarts, and you need plenty of depth so that the muffins can puff up like little chef's hats.

Sift the flour with the baking powder into a bowl and mix in the cornmeal, sugar and a pinch of salt. Make a well in the middle with your fist. When the buttery milk has cooled to finger heat, pour it into the hollow in the flour mixture. Tip the egg into the milk and stir everything together until well blended and free of lumps. Fold in the blueberries.

Spoon the mixture into the buttered muffin tin – it should come about two thirds of the way up each hole.

Bake the muffins for 20–25 minutes until they're well risen and the tops are golden brown. Transfer to a wire rack to cool.

Makes about 12

250ml milk
125g butter, roughly chopped
125g plain flour
2 teaspoons baking powder
250g fine-ground cornmeal
2 tablespoons sugar
salt
1 organic free-range egg, forked
   to blend
2 heaped tablespoons fresh
   blueberries

You need a small saucepan, a muffin tin with 12 deep holes, a mixing bowl and sieve, a wooden spoon, a small bowl and fork and a metal spoon. This recipe uses both the top of the stove and the oven.

cup cakes

First-time cooks can whip up a cake 'batter' with dry rice and lentils plus a few sugar sprinkles for fun, and then help decorate the real cakes when they're baked. Older and more experienced kitchen-collaborators can do it all without any help.

Makes about 12

180g unsalted butter, softened
180g caster sugar
180g plain flour
1 teaspoon baking powder
3 medium organic free-range eggs

To finish
about 4 tablespoons icing sugar
sugar sprinkles

You need 2 mixing bowls, a sieve, a wooden spoon and a metal spoon, about 12 cup-cake cases and a baking sheet. We used heatproof plastic cupcake cases, which don't collapse. Paper ones can be supported by dropping them in a 12-hole tart tin. This recipe uses the oven.

Put the softened butter in a warm mixing bowl with the caster sugar and beat it with a wooden spoon until it's really light and pale. Or use an electric mixer.

Sift the flour with the baking powder into another bowl.

Crack the eggs into a cup, one at a time, and beat each egg into the butter and sugar, still using the wooden spoon and adding a little flour if the mixture looks like splitting. Change spoons: you need a metal one for the next step. Mix in the rest of the flour carefully, adding it spoonful by spoonful and turning the mixture over and over to blend it thoroughly – there should be no little pockets of white flour when you've finished.

Preheat the oven to 190°C/375°F/gas mark 5.

Meanwhile, arrange 12 paper cup-cake cases on a baking sheet. Spoon the batter into the cases carefully – don't fill them right to the top.

Bake for 25–30 minutes – check after 20 minutes – until well risen, brown and firm. Use your nose and your ears when the oven's open: the cakes will smell all buttery and delicious, and when they're ready, they stop hissing.

Allow the cakes to cool in their cases and ice them as soon as they're cool. Mix the icing sugar with enough cold water to make a trickling cream. A few sugar sprinkles will finish the cakes off nicely.

Frances says: The first job I ever had was making my dad's packed lunch every day. I decided what to make, shopped for what I needed, kept to a budget, and at the end of the week, he paid me my wages and told me how much he liked what I'd cooked – which taught me how important it is for children to have something good to take to school. So here are 12 great lunchbox recipes – wraps, fistfuls, cakes and cookies – plus a tasty after-school snack.

off to school

Elisabeth says: Packed lunches mean different things in different parts of the world: all they have in common is that they must be easy to carry and taste good even when they've cooled. In great-granny's day, when all country children walked to school, everyone knew which wild leaves, berries and nuts could be nibbled along the way, adding a healthy dose of fresh greens and fruit to the day's intake, plus the exercise that came with the territory.

9

asparagus and potato tortilla

tortilla de asparagos trigueros

In Spain, a packed lunch usually includes a wedge of Spanish omelette, a firm, juicy egg-cake in which potato provides the bulk. This version includes a few spears of fresh green asparagus, though you can leave it plain or include anything else you fancy that will add interest. The only rule is that all additions must be fully cooked before they're mixed with the egg. Other favourite extras are green beans, slivered artichoke hearts, diced red peppers, cubes of serrano ham or chorizo.

Chop the asparagus into bite-sized pieces. Peel and dice the potatoes, or cut them into thin slivers or chips. Crack the eggs into a bowl and fork them up with the salt – they should be well blended but not frothy. The volume of the additions should equal that of the egg: when you've prepared the vegetables, measure roughly by eye.

In a small frying pan heat enough oil to submerge the potatoes completely – a French omelette pan is just the right size and shape. As soon as the oil is lightly hazed with blue, add the potatoes and fry them gently until soft – don't let them brown – then transfer with a draining spoon to a sieve set over a bowl to catch the drippings. Fry the asparagus pieces for no more than a minute – just enough to heat them through. Transfer the asparagus to the sieve with the potato and tip everything, including the drippings, into the egg, turning to blend.

Tip out all but 1 tablespoon of oil from the pan. Reheat the pan and pour in the egg mixture. Cook gently – high heat makes eggs leathery – lifting the edges to allow the uncooked egg to run underneath. You can speed up the setting process by placing a lid on the pan. When the egg begins to look set in the middle – 3–4 minutes – shake the pan to make sure the tortilla base is loose.

Remove from the heat. Now, with the handle in one hand and a plate in the other, place the plate face-side down on the pan and reverse the whole thing in one quick movement. Replace the pan on the heat, add a little more oil and slip in the tortilla, this time with the soft side downwards. Be brave – it's easy; if you're nervous at first, put a cloth over your arm to protect you from oily drips. Cook the other side for a further 2–3 minutes, neatening the sides with a spatula to build up a firm edge. The middle should still be juicy and the outside perfectly firm. Tip the tortilla out on to kitchen paper, pat off the excess oil, allow to cool to room temperature and cut into neat quarters or squares.

Serves 4 children

4–5 thin green asparagus spears, trimmed
2 large potatoes
3 large organic free-range eggs
½ teaspoon salt
oil for frying

For balance, sliced oranges and bread – no Spaniard would dream of a meal without bread.

Indonesian coconut rice rolls
lempur

In tropical regions where the heat is fierce during the day, children attend school from early morning until it's time for the midday meal, taking a snack to bridge the gap. In its simplest form, this is a helping of coconut rice with a little flavouring dip of spices and dried powdered shrimp (*blacan*) to be mixed in with the fingers. In the old days the wrapping was a banana leaf, replaced in modern times by a plastic box, depriving children, say those who remember their own schooldays, of the subtle flavour of the leaves as well as the pleasure of unwrapping the parcel. If you can't find banana leaves, use baking foil or parchment.

Makes 12

Put the rice in a heavy saucepan with the coconut milk and salt, bring to the boil, turn the heat right down, lid tightly and cook very gently for 20 minutes, until the rice is tender and the liquid has all been absorbed. If it still looks damp, stir round the edges with a fork, and cook uncovered for a further 5 minutes. Set aside to cool.

For the rice
2 cups glutinous rice (*ketan*) or any round-grain rice
1 litre coconut milk
½ teaspoon salt
oil for brushing

You're now ready to assemble the parcels.

Preheat the oven to 180°C/350°F/gas mark 4.

Cut a sheet of baking foil or parchment into rectangles about the length and width of your hand. Lay the squares on the table and brush the middle of each square with a little oil.

For the filling
1 firm avocado, cut into batons
juice of 1 lime
1 small slice fresh ginger, matchsticked
12 small sprigs of coriander

Lay 1 heaped tablespoon of the rice on each wrapper, using the back of the spoon to make a dip in the middle. Place a piece of avocado, a sprinkle of lime juice, a scrap of ginger and a sprig of coriander in each dip, and mould the rice over the filling to form a little cylinder. Fold the wrapper over the cylinder, tucking in the sides halfway through the rolling to make a neat parcel.

For balance, toasted shredded coconut and chunked papaya.

Transfer the parcels to a baking sheet and bake for 15 minutes until heated through – test with your finger – to allow the rice to take the flavour of the filling. Remove and leave to cool to room temperature.

slow-cooked beef with wine and olives
daube de boeuf provençale

Thermos food – something soupy and spoonable which keeps its heat without drying out – is a good way to provide a hot meal to eat at school on a cold day. The traditional French daube is a robust beef stew cooked with the rough red wine of Provence – no need to worry about the alcohol as it evaporates during the first few minutes of cooking, leaving the wine to deepen the flavour and help to tenderise the meat.

A daube was the traditional Sunday dinner in the cold uplands of the Languedoc where my children attended school some 30 years ago. The youngest was at the local nursery school – école maternelle. She took her lunch in a canteen, an enamel bucket with a sealable lid. In the bottom was a ladleful of daube or some other soupy stew and on the top was a little metal dish for the hors d'oeuvre: olives, celeriac in mustardy mayonnaise, grated carrot, a little tomato salad. The dinner lady collected all the canteens as the children arrived, removed the hors d'oeuvres and set them at each child's place, resealed the containers and popped them in a big pot of boiling water to heat up for the midday break. The school provided fresh bread and water, and everyone ate heartily and well.

Drop the meat into a plastic or paper bag with the seasoned flour and shake to coat. Heat the oil in a flameproof casserole, add the meat and toss over the heat for 4–5 minutes till it browns a little on all sides. Remove and reserve. Add the bacon, shallots or onions and carrot to the casserole and fry till everything sizzles and takes a little colour. Return the meat to the casserole and add the olives, orange zest, cinnamon, peppercorns, thyme and bay. Add the red wine and enough water to submerge the meat – about 500ml – and bubble it up, stirring to avoid sticking, till the steam no longer smells of alcohol.

Turn down the heat, lid the pot securely (seal it with a flour-and-water paste if the fit isn't perfect) and either simmer very gently on a low heat or transfer to a medium oven, 170°C/325°F/gas mark 3. Cook for 1½–2 hours till the meat is so tender it can be eaten with a spoon. You may need to add a little more water towards the end of cooking, to prevent it drying out. Check the seasoning – you may want a little sugar to balance the acidity of the wine, but you shouldn't need extra salt as the bacon and olives provide plenty.

Serves 12 children and 2 adults

1kg stewing beef, trimmed and diced
1 tablespoon seasoned flour
2 tablespoons olive oil
2 tablespoons diced bacon (include the rind)
500g shallots or pickling onions, peeled
4 garlic cloves, skinned and crushed
1 large carrot, scraped and diced
1 tablespoon black olives
2–3 curls dried orange zest (see below)
1 short piece cinnamon stick
½ teaspoon crushed peppercorns
1 sprig of thyme
1–2 bay leaves
500ml young red wine (nothing grand)
salt and pepper

For balance, a chunk of fresh baguette and a little pot of fruit-flavoured yogurt.

To prepare your own dried orange zest, pare the zest from a large orange and set it to dry for a week or two in the sun on a windowsill.

meatballs in bulgur
kibbeh

Spiced minced meat enclosed in a thin shell of cracked wheat, Lebanon's favourite finger food takes time, patience and a great deal of skill. This somewhat rough-and-ready version from the Dominican Republic (blame an influx of Lebanese immigrants) is quick and it works.

Put the bulgur in a bowl and pour in enough boiling water to cover the grains to a depth of one finger. Stir and leave to swell for 1 hour.

Meanwhile, fry the meat with the onion – you may need a little oil – until all the juices have evaporated and the meat begins to brown. Sprinkle in the parsley and cinnamon and season with the salt and pepper. Turn well to blend, remove from the heat and set aside to cool.

When the bulgur has absorbed all the moisture, mix half into the meat mixture and work it with your hands or in a food-processor until it's firm enough to hold together. Have a bowl of warm water by your side to dampen your hands and work the mixture into 12 small, torpedo-shaped balls. Roll the balls in the remaining bulgur, pressing to coat. Transfer to a baking sheet lined with clingfilm. Repeat until all the ingredients are used up and you have neat little rows of torpedoes, each just enough for two bites. Leave to set for 30 minutes, or overnight in the fridge.

In a frying pan, heat enough oil to submerge the kibbeh. When the oil smokes a little, slip them in – not too many at a time – and fry, turning carefully, until perfectly golden and crisp, about 6–7 minutes. Transfer to kitchen paper to drain.

Makes 12

250g fine bulgur (cracked wheat)

For the filling
500g minced lamb
oil for frying
1 medium onion, peeled and grated
1 tablespoon chopped parsley
1 teaspoon powdered cinnamon
1 teaspoon salt
½ teaspoon pepper

For balance, cucumber sticks and fresh or dried apricots, with a handful of almonds for nibbling.

ham and tomato pasties
pastelitos de jamón

Makes 12

For the filling
2 tablespoons olive oil
1 onion, peeled and finely chopped
1 garlic clove, skinned and crushed
500g ripe tomatoes, skinned,
deseeded and diced
1 teaspoon oregano
100g ham or lean bacon, diced
250g diced pumpkin or chayote

For the pastry
350g strong white bread flour
1 teaspoon baking powder
½ teaspoon salt
4 tablespoons oil
4 tablespoons milk
about 150ml boiling water

For balance, tropical fruit:
pineapple chunks or
the small, sweet, juicy
Windward Isles bananas.

The mid-morning snack – merienda – a child takes to school in a tropical climate such as that of the Caribbean needs to be something which won't become inedible in the heat. Salt-cured pork products such as ham and chorizo fit the bill because the method of curing ensures that the meat has no need of refrigeration.

To make the filling, heat the oil in a frying pan and gently fry the onion and garlic until they soften – 3–4 minutes. Add the diced tomatoes and oregano and a spoonful of cold water, bubble up again, reduce the heat and cook gently for 5–10 minutes, mashing with a wooden spoon, until the tomatoes collapse and the sauce thickens. Stir in the ham or bacon and the diced pumpkin or chayote and bubble up again until the vegetable softens. Remove the pan from the heat and set aside to cool while you mix the pastry. A hot-water crust has to be used while it's still warm – no resting time required.

Preheat the oven to 200°C/400°F/gas mark 6.

Sift the flour, baking powder and salt into a bowl and make a well in the middle. In a jug, mix the oil and milk with the boiling water and pour it into the well. Work the dry and wet ingredients together until you have a soft, sticky dough. Knead it until smooth and elastic; don't take too long, as the dough should be worked while it's warm. Form it into a roll and chop it into 12 equal pieces. Roll out each piece into a thin disc with a lightly floured rolling pin, or pat out between 2 sheets of clingfilm. Put a teaspoon of the filling into the centre of each disc. Wet the edges with a damp finger and fold one half over the other to enclose the filling. Mark the edges with a fork to seal. Transfer the pasties to an oiled baking sheet.

Bake for about 15 minutes, until the pastry is golden and crisp. Transfer to a wire rack to cool.

Cornish pasties

Makes 4 child-sized pasties

For the pastry
350g strong white bread flour
½ teaspoon salt
75g lard, frozen
75g butter, frozen
4–5 tablespoons cold water

For the filling
125g onion, peeled and sliced
into fine half moons
250g turnip, peeled and
matchsticked
350g lean beef, slivered
across the grain
500g potatoes, peeled and
matchsticked
salt and pepper

For balance, a crisp apple
or a well-scrubbed carrot.

Cold-water pastry like this
must be kept cold throughout
its preparation or it'll be
heavy. A hot-water pastry, like
that used for the Caribbean
ham and tomato pasties on
the previous page, must not be
allowed to cool or it will
crumble and collapse.

The Cornish tin-miner's traditional midday break was also tucked in the pocket of Cornish schoolchildren in the days when everyone walked to school. The size of the pasty depends on the size of the person, but one pasty should be enough to satisfy the pangs of hunger all day. It was the custom to mark each pasty with an initial, so that there was no mistaking which one was yours.

Make the pastry first. Everything should be as cold as possible. Sift the flour with the salt into a bowl and leave it in the fridge for 1–2 hours.

When the flour is really cold, grate in the fat and stir it in with a knife. Mix in enough cold water to make a manageable dough. Knead it for a moment, but not for long. The fat should remain quite lumpy, to give a firm enough crust to hold the juices of the filling. Cover the dough ball with clingfilm and leave it in the fridge for at least 30 minutes.

Preheat the oven to 200°C/400°F/gas mark 6.

Divide the dough into 4 equal pieces and roll each piece out on a floured board into rounds the size of a saucer. Drop a little onion into the middle of each round, top with a layer of turnip, then with meat, then with potato, seasoning as you go and making sure the filling will reach right into the ends when you make your parcels.

Dampen the pastry edges with a wet finger, then bring the sides together over the top to form a fat bolster. Pinch the edges together firmly, starting at the middle and finishing at the corners. Dry your fingers, then crimp the pinched edge between your thumb and forefinger to form a rope – the seal needs to be perfect. Transfer the pasties to a non-stick baking sheet; don't prick or slit them.

Bake for 15 minutes in the hot oven to crisp and brown the pastry, then turn the oven down to 180°C/350°F/gas mark 4, lay a sheet of foil on top of the pasties, shiny side down, and continue baking for a further 25 minutes to cook the insides.

If you're baking them in the morning, they can be cooked while the family eats breakfast. Pop each pasty into its own paper bag and it'll stay warm until the midday break.

oatcakes with cream crowdie

Fine-ground oatmeal gives a smooth, crisp Scottish oatcake to eat with cream cheese – crowdie. Make sure you have proper milled oatmeal – rolled porridge oats won't do.

Preheat the oven to 150°C/300°F/gas mark 2 or set a griddle to heat.

In a roomy bowl, mix the oatmeal with the salt. Mash in the shortening – dripping, lard or butter – with a fork or your fingers. Work in enough warm water to make a firm dough. Form it into a ball and pat it out between 2 sheets of clingfilm until it's about 3mm thick. Cut into rounds with a sharp-edged wine glass or pastry cutter.

If you're using the oven, transfer the rounds to a lightly greased baking sheet, and bake for 30–40 minutes, until the oatcakes look dry and crisp and a little brown at the edges; don't let them take colour all over. Transfer carefully to a wire rack and leave to cool.

If you're using a griddle, wipe it over with a scrap of clean cloth dipped in dripping or butter, and test the heat with a sprinkle of flour: the grains should turn golden by the time you've counted to ten. Transfer the oatcakes to the hot surface and bake gently until dry and lightly browned at the edges. Stack the oatcakes in a rack in front of the heat to dry them off completely.

Store them buried in a jar of oatmeal, or wrapped in a clean cloth in a tin. If the oatcakes soften in storage, warm them up again in a gentle oven: they'll crisp as they cool. Take them to school as a mid-morning snack to eat with the crowdie – a piece for the pocket, as they say in Scotland.

Makes about 24 oatcakes

500g fine-ground oatmeal
½ teaspoon salt
2 tablespoons dripping or
    lard or butter
about 300ml warm water

To serve
50g cream cheese per person

For balance, a punnet of Scottish raspberries or a crunchy apple.

cut-and-come-again cake

Makes a 1.5kg cake

For the first cooking:
175g currants
175g raisins
100g brown sugar
2 tablespoons vinegar
2 tablespoons water

For the second cooking:
500g plain flour
2 teaspoons baking powder
50g caster sugar
100g butter
200ml buttermilk

For balance,
Cheddar cheese and
a Cox's Orange Pippin.

An old-fashioned English nursery recipe, this'll keep for months in a tin, which is why it got its name. The cake-batter is cooked twice – first boiled, then baked.

Put the first-cooking ingredients into a small pan. Stir, transfer to the heat and simmer gently for 10 minutes, stirring occasionally, then remove and leave to cool.

Preheat the oven to 200°C/400°F/gas mark 6.

Meanwhile, sift the flour and baking powder into a bowl and mix in the sugar. Rub in the butter until the mixture is like fine breadcrumbs. Stir in enough buttermilk to give a firm batter. Fold in the cooled fruit mixture.

Pour the batter into a 1.5kg loaf tin lined with baking parchment.

Bake in the hot oven for 20 minutes, then reduce the heat to 170°C/325°F/gas mark 3 and bake for a further 30–40 minutes, until the cake is well risen and firm; keep an eye on it and cover it with foil (shiny side upwards, to deflect the heat) if the top browns too fast. Transfer to a wire rack to cool. Remove the paper before you store it in a tin.

Welshcakes

Halfway between biscuits and scones, these are the treat at the bottom of a Welsh schoolchild's lunch-box. They're easy to make and even easier to eat.

Rub the butter into the flour and add the raisins and sugar. Mix the water with the eggs and add to the dry ingredients to make a soft dough. Tip on to a well-floured board and roll it out to a thickness of 1cm. Cut into rounds with a sharp-edged water glass or a 6cm shell-edged cutter.

Heat the griddle or a heavy frying pan gently and thoroughly – don't let it overheat.

Slip the cakes on to the hot metal and wait until the underside browns and the top begins to dry – about 4–5 minutes.. Turn gently to cook the other side. Transfer to a clean cloth to cool. Store in an airtight tin.

Makes 24

25g butter
500g self-raising flour
2 tablespoons raisins
100g sugar
200ml water
2 large organic free-range eggs

For balance,
vegetable soup in
a Thermos.

paradise cookies
croquantes de granos de paraíso

These crisp little cookies pack an unusual punch since they include amaranth seeds, an important food source for the Aztecs. Modern Mexicans know them as *granos de paraíso*, seeds of paradise, and include them in nut brittles as well as in crisp buttery cookies. They are sold as after-school snacks at dozens of road-side kiosks, along with a paper cone of fresh fruit prepared to order and offered with a shake of chilli powder instead of sugar.

Makes about 24

150g plain flour
2 tablespoons amaranth seeds
100g butter
50g sugar

To finish
walnut or pecan halves

For balance, tropical fruit: chunks of watermelon for the juiciness you need in a hot climate, passion fruit for portability and the excitement of biting into the leathery skin and sucking out the pulp.

Sift the flour into a mixing bowl and mix in the amaranth seeds. Beat the butter with the sugar until light and white. Using the tips of your fingers, work in enough of the flour mixture to make a soft dough – stop before it goes crumbly. Press the dough lightly into a ball, still using the tips of your fingers, and roll it in clingfilm. Set in a cool place to rest for 20–30 minutes for the seeds and flour to swell.

Preheat the oven to 150°C/300°F/gas mark 2.

Dust a board or clean work surface with a little flour, drop on the dough ball and flatten it to make a thick round – remove the clingfilm first, then replace it when the dough-ball has been flattened. Roll or pat out to the thickness of your thumb. Cut out small rounds with a biscuit cutter or sharp-edged drinking glass and transfer to a buttered baking sheet lightly dusted with flour. Gather the scraps together, pat out again and continue until the dough is all used up. Make a dent in the top of each cookie with a damp finger and press in a half walnut or pecan.

Bake for 30–40 minutes. The cookies will spread as they cook – don't worry, just let 'em wander. Remove when they're nicely browned at the edges; they'll crisp as they cool. Transfer to a wire rack as soon as they harden a little, and allow to cool completely before you break them into convenient pieces. They keep well in an airtight tin.

Honey and almond shortbreads (see page 000) and paradise cookies

honey and almond shortbreads
kourabiedes

Olive oil is used instead of butter in these nutty little cinnamon-flavoured cookies – nuts provide the protein, honey serves as the sweetener. Well, nobody's perfect.

Makes about 24

225g plain flour
1 teaspoon powdered cinnamon
100g ground almonds
1 teaspoon finely grated
orange zest
175g light olive oil
100g runny honey
1 organic free-range egg,
forked to blend

For balance, olives and cheese: kefalotiri and feta are good and Greek.

Sift the flour with the cinnamon into a roomy bowl, then mix in the ground almonds and the orange zest.

Beat the olive oil with the honey until well blended, then beat it into the flour, adding enough egg to form a ball of soft dough which just holds its shape – you may need to use less egg or add a little water. Or drop everything in a food-processor and process until the dough forms into a single lump.

Cover the dough with clingfilm and leave it to rest and firm in the fridge for 1 hour.

Preheat the oven to 210°C/425°F/gas mark 7.

On a lightly floured board, roll the dough out to the thickness of your little finger. Using a biscuit cutter or sharp-edged wine glass, cut out bite-sized rounds and transfer them to a buttered, lightly floured baking sheet. Press the scraps together with your fingertips to form a ball, pat out and cut, and repeat until all the dough is used up.

Bake the shortbreads for 15–20 minutes until they're pale gold and perfectly dry.

Swedish butter-cookies
smörkaker

Little ring-shaped cookies spiced with cardamom, a popular flavouring for sweet things in Scandinavia. Cardamom flavours the Christmas dessert, a creamy rice pudding, and is included in the spice-mix for gingerbread, pepperkaker.

Beat the butter with the sugar until fluffy and pale. Beat in the lemon juice and zest. Sift in the flour, add the cardamom and beat with a wooden spoon until you have a smooth soft dough – you'll probably need a spoonful or two of cold water. Or do the whole thing in a food-processor.

Form the dough into a ball, cover with clingfilm and set it in the fridge for 1–2 hours to rest and firm. Turn the dough ball out on to a lightly floured pastry board, flatten it with little pats of the rolling pin and roll it out into a rectangle about 30 x 10cm. Cut it into 10cm strips about as wide as your little finger.

Preheat the oven to 180°C/350°F/gas mark 4.

Twist 2 of the pastry strips together and join them into a ring with a dampened finger. Continue until all the strips are formed into pairs and rings. Arrange on a well-buttered baking sheet and bake for about 10 minutes until golden. Transfer to a wire rack to cool. Store in an airtight tin.

Makes about 30

400g unsalted butter, softened
300g caster sugar
juice and finely grated zest
   of 1 lemon 475g plain flour
1 teaspoon crushed
   cardamom seeds

For balance, pea
soup in a Thermos.

pancake soup

frittensuppe

Serves 2 children and 2 adults

1 litre strong beef broth
(see right)

For the pancakes
3 organic free-range eggs
250g flour
about 250ml milk
salt
grated nutmeg
butter for frying

To finish
chopped parsley or chives

There's nothing like a steaming bowl of soup as a pick-me-up after a long day in a cold schoolroom. Austrian children count themselves lucky to come home to a bowl of *frittensuppe*, clear beef-bone broth with pancake ribbons added in much the same way as noodles. Parsley is the only additional flavouring. Serve all three elements separately for freedom of choice.

For 1 litre of beef broth – enough for 2 children and 2 adults – you need 4 segments of sawn-up marrow bones. Beef shin or osso bucco can replace the marrow bones – allow 500g, tied in a piece. Roast in a hot oven, transfer to a large boiling pot and add a handful of diced root vegetables – parsley root, carrot, onion, leek – and a few allspice berries. Add enough water to cover generously and simmer for at least an hour. In a pressure cooker, 10 minutes is all it needs. Strain, discarding the solids, and bubble up until it is reduced to 1 litre. Don't skim off all the little globules of golden fat: they add richness and confirm that the broth is home-made.

Heat the broth while you make the pancakes. Whisk the eggs, flour and milk thoroughly in a jug until you have a smooth, pourable cream, and season with a little salt and nutmeg. Or put everything in a food-processor and whizz to a cream.

Melt a nugget of butter in a pancake pan – a small frying pan with a very smooth surface. As soon as the butter froths, pour in a little of the batter, just enough to coat the base of the pan, and swirl it around to spread the mixture evenly. When the pancake's dry on top, it's ready to turn. Flip it over and cook the other side. Repeat until all the batter is used up. Pile up the pancakes in a clean cloth as you go. When all the pancakes are cooked, cut the pile right through in quarters, and slice the quarters into fine strips like tagliatelle.

Ladle the broth into soup bowls and finish each portion with pancake strips and a sprinkle of parsley or chives.

index

açorda de mariscos 56
addas pillau 50
Afghanistan
  lamb korma with cardamom 84
Africa see Morocco; Senegal;
  South Africa
aligot 77
all-pork sausages 86
anginares ladolemono 34
apple
  apple & cinnamon drop-
    scones 71
  apple purée 15
artichokes with oil & lemon 34
asparagus
  asparagi al uovo 37
  asparagus & potato tortilla 141
  asparagus with eggs 37
aubergine
  baked aubergine & lamb 60
Austria
  pancake soup 156
avocado with tortilla crisps
  & black beans 43

bacon
  lettuce & bacon soup 69
  old clothes 87
baked aubergine & lamb 60
banana
  banana bread with cinnamon
    & pecans 73
  mangu 27
barley
  lemon barley water 25
  Scotch broth 40
basil
  bean soup with basil 76
  beach party paella 72
bean soup with basil 76
beancurd
  miso soup with beancurd118
beans
  avocado with tortilla chips
    & black beans 43
  bean soup with basil 76
  butterbeans with greens 32
  Dominican kidney beans &
    rice 96
beef
  beef & carrot hotpot 59
  Cornish pasties 148
  pancake soup 156
  slow-cooked beef with wine
    & olives 143
Belgium
  leek purée 12
  mussels with oven chips 79
blueberries
  blueberry corn-muffins 135

blueberry soup 12
boreki 131
bowl food 17–21
bratwurst 86
bread
  bread & tomato 20
  bread pudding with cheese
    & ham 57
  bread risotto with seafood 56
  fattoush 129
  Parisian pain au chocolat 125
  pull-aparts 132
Britain
  Cornish pasties 148
  Scotch broth 40
  Welshcakes 151
broccoli
  fairy-dust 65
  paper-wrapped chicken with
    steamed broccoli 109
broths see purées & broths
bulgur
  meatballs in bulgur 145
butterbeans with greens 32
butternut squash
  quinoa & butternut squash 19

Caribbean
  ham & tomato pasties 146
  mangu 27
calamares a la romana 36
cardamom
  lamb korma with cardamom 84
carrot
  beef & carrot hotpot 59
  potatoes & carrots 24
  winter minestrone 41
celery
  winter minestrone 41
chapatis with potato &
  spinach curry 111
cheese
  bread pudding with cheese
    & ham 57
  cheese filo-pastry pie 99
  cheesy potatoes 77
  fairy-dust 65
  fisherman's piece-for-the-
    pocket 66
  fresh egg-noodles with
    cheese 45
  olives, ham & cheese 33
  pasta with pumpkin &
    ricotta 64
  spinach & cheese parcels 131
chicken
  beach party paella 72
  chicken rice with lemongrass
    & lime leaves 81
  chicken soup with rice 24
  chicken with rice & egg 53
  fried chicken with onions 103
  garlic chicken 82
  Indonesian satay 102
  paper-wrapped chicken with

steamed broccoli 109
chickpeas
  chickpea fritters with sesame
    sauce 94
  chickpea stew with chorizo 55
  Friday couscous with chickpea
    stew 116
Chile
  butterbeans with greens 32
China
  paper-wrapped chicken with
    steamed broccoli 109
  rice congee 14
  table manners 110
chocolate
  Parisian pain au chocolat 125
chorizo
  chickpea stew with chorizo 55
Cinderella's midnight feast 64
cinnamon
  pork braised with cinnamon
    & onions 85
  princess-and-the-pea
    pancakes 71
  treehouse picnic 73
cocido con chorizo 55
coconut milk
  rice noodles with coconut
    milk & prawns 48
  yellow rice with coconut
    milk 51
cooking together 120–137
Cornish pasties 148
cornmeal see polenta
couscous 114
  Friday couscous with chickpea
    stew 116
crispbread with soured milk
  & raspberries 122
croquantes de granos de paraiso
  152
cucumber
  Swedish cold table 114
cup cakes 136
cut-and-come-again cake 150
dates
  saffron rice with lentils &
    dates 50
daube de boeuf provençale 143
Denmark
  blueberry soup 12
  pea purée 15
Dominican Republic
  Dominican kidney beans &
    rice 96
  mangu 27
  meatballs in bulgur 145
Dr Bircher's Swiss muesli 124

eggs
  asparagus & potato tortilla 141
  asparagus with eggs 37
  herb omelette 106
  fairy-dust 65
falafel bin tahini 94

fattoush 129
fideu a la catalana 47
fireman's lunch 69
first-aid foods 22–27
fish & seafood
  bread risotto with seafood 56
  frittered calamares 36
  mussels with oven chips 79
  Norwegian fish patties 101
  pirate's breakfast 68
  rice noodles with coconut
    milk & prawns 48
  Swedish cold table 114
  fisherman's piece-for-the-
    pocket 66
fiskekaker 101
France
  bean soup with basil 76
  cheesy potatoes 77
  French hazelnut nutella 124
  garlic broth 27
  herb omelette 106
  olives, ham, cheese 33
  Parisian pain au chocolat 125
  slow-cooked beef with wine
    & olives 143
  table manners 107
French hazelnut nutella 124
Friday couscous with chickpea
  stew 116
fried chicken with onions 103
frittensuppe 156
frittered calamares 36

garlic
  chickpea soup with chorizo 55
  garlic broth 27
  garlic chicken 82
Germany
  all-pork sausages 86
  fresh egg-noodles with cheese
    45
Greece
  artichokes with oil & lemon 34
  baked aubergine & lamb 60
  pork braised with cinnamon
    & onions 85
greens
  butterbeans with greens 32
  greens with peanuts 95
  old clothes 87
  grilled pork chops 69
guacamole con nachos y frijoles 43

habichuelas con arroz 96
ham
  beach party paella 72
  bread pudding with cheese
    & ham 57
  ham & tomato pasties 146
  old clothes 87
  olives, ham, cheese 33
harira 90
herb omelette 106
hirino stifado 85

Holland
  beef & carrot hotpot 59
honey & almond shortbreads
  154
hot 'n' sour fishcakes 68
Hungary
  blueberry soup 12
  lamb goulash 61
hutspot 59

India
  chapatis with potato &
    spinach curry 111
  red lentils with spinach 20
  table manners 113
Indonesia
  hot 'n' sour fishcakes 68
  Indonesian coconut rice
    rolls 142
  Indonesian satay 102
  yellow rice with coconut milk
    51
Iran
  saffron rice with lentils &
    dates 50
Italy
  asparagus with eggs 37
  bread & tomato 20
  bread pudding with cheese
    & ham 57
  fisherman's piece-for-the-
    pocket 66
  Ligurian focaccia 126
  macaroni with wild rabbit 46
  Neapolitan calzone 127
  olives, ham, cheese 33
  rags-and-tatters 128
  Tuscan winter minestrone 41

jambalaya 52
Japan
  Japanese noodles with tahini
    dressing 91
  miso soup with beancurd 118
  table manners 119
Java see Indonesia
junket 14

khao man kai 81
kibbeh 145
korma chalau 84
köttbullar 80

laksa lemak 48
lamb
  baked aubergine & lamb 60
  lamb goulash 61
  lamb korma with cardamom 84
  meatballs in bulgur 145
  Scotch broth 40
Latin America
  ham & tomato pasties 146
  sweet potato purée 16
  see also Chile; Dominican
    Republic; Mexico; Peru

Lebanon
  meatballs in bulgar wheat 145
  Ramadan lentil soup 90
leek purée 12
lemon barley water 25
lemongrass
  chicken rice with lemongrass
    & lime leaves 81
lempur 142
lentils
  Ramadan lentil soup 90
  red lentils with spinach 20
  saffron rice with lentils &
    dates 50
lettuce & bacon soup 69
Ligurian focaccia 126
lima beans *see* butter beans
lime leaves
  chicken rice with lemongrass
    & lime leaves 81
limeños con espinacas 32
Louisiana jambalaya 52

macaroni with wild rabbit 46
maccharoni alla cacciatora 46
mamaliga 19
mangu 27
meatballs
  in bulgar wheat 145
  with cream sauce 80
Mexico
  avocado with tortilla crisps
    & black beans 43
  paradise cookies 152
Middle East
  falafel with tahini 94
  Middle Eastern bread salad 129
  see also Iran; Lebanon
miso soup with beancurd 118
monkfish
  bread risotto with seafood 56
Morocco
  couscous bin tagine 116
  table manners 117
moules frites 79
mozzarella
  fisherman's piece-for-the-
    pocket 66
msamba 95
mussels with oven chips 79

nasi kuning 51
Neapolitan calzone 127
nem 98
Netherlands *see* Holland
New Orleans granola 125
noodles
  Japanese noodles with tahini
    dressing 91
  Singapore fried noodles 92
North America
  grilled pork chops 69
  Louisiana jambalaya 52
  New Orleans granola
    125

Norway
  crispbread with soured milk
    & raspberries 122
  Norwegian fish patties 101
nuts & seeds
  Dr Bircher's Swiss muesli 124
  French hazelnut nutella 124
  greens with peanuts 95
  New Orleans granola 125
  paradise cookies 152
  poppy-seed dumplings 44
  treehouse picnic 73

oatcakes with cream crowdie
  149
oats & oatmeal
  Dr Bircher's Swiss muesli 124
  New Orleans granola 125
  oatcakes with cream crowdie
    149
old clothes 87
olives, ham, cheese 33
omelette fines herbes 106
onion
  fried chicken with onions 103
  Ligurian focaccia 126
  pork braised with cinnamon
    & onions 85
oyako donburi 53

paella 72
panada alla parmigiana 57
pancake soup 156
papa al pomodoro 20
paper-wrapped chicken with
  steamed broccoli 109
papoutsakia 60
paprikas 61
paradise cookies 152
Parisian *pain au chocolat* 125
pasta
  macaroni with wild rabbit 46
  pasta with pork 47
  pasta with pumpkin &
    ricotta 64
  winter minestrone 41
pastelitos de jamón 146
pastry
  cheese filo-pastry pie 99
  ham & tomato pasties 146
  spinach & cheese parcels 131
pea purée 15
peanuts
  greens with peanuts 95
  Indonesian satay 102
pecans 73
Peru
  quinoa & butternut squash 19
pirate's breakfast 68
piroshki 44
pita sa kajmak 99
pizza 126, 127
plantain
  mangu 27
Poland
  poppy-seed dumplings 44
Romania

polenta with yogurt 19
pollo al ajillo 82
poppy-seed dumplings 44
pork
  all-pork sausages 86
  fireman's lunch 69
  Louisiana jambalaya 52
  meatballs with cream sauce 80
  pasta with pork 47
  pork braised with cinnamon
    & onions 85
Portugal
  bread risotto with seafood 56
  old clothes 87
potato
  asparagus & potato tortilla 141
  beef & carrot hotpot 59
  chapatis with potato &
    spinach curry 111
  cheesy potatoes 77
  Cornish pasties 148
  old clothes 87
  potatoes & carrots 24
  Scotch broth 40
  Swedish cold table 114
prawns 48
  rice noodles with coconut
    milk & prawns 48
presentation of food 30
princess-and-the-pea pancakes 71
prune compote 24
pull-aparts 132
pumpkin
  Cinderella's midnight feast 64
purées & broths 10–16

quinoa & butternut squash 19

rabbit
  macaroni with wild rabbit 46
rags-and-tatters 128
Ramadan lentil soup 90
raspberries
  crispbread with soured milk
    & raspberries 122
  red lentils with spinach 20
rice
  beach party paella 72
  fisherman's piece-for-the-
    pocket 66
  Indonesian coconut rice rolls
    142
  Louisiana jambalaya 52
  paper-wrapped chicken with
    steamed broccoli 109
  rice congee 14
  rice noodles with coconut
    milk & prawns 48
  saffron rice with lentils &
    dates 50
  yellow rice with coconut
    milk 51
rice-wrapper rolls 98
ricotta 64
Romania

blueberry soup 12
polenta with yogurt 19
roupa velha 87
saffron rice with chicken &
  ham 72
saffron rice with lentils &
  dates 50
sage & onion pizza-bread 126
salmon
  Swedish cold table 114
salt-cod
  bread risotto with seafood 56
sausages
  all-pork sausages 86
Scandinavia
  blueberry soup 12
  table manners 115
  see also Denmark; Norway;
    Sweden
scent, dishes characterised by
  75–87
school lunches & after-school
  food 138–155
Scotch broth 40
seafood *see* fish & seafood
Senegal
  fried chicken with onions 103
Serbia
  cheese filo-pastry pie 99
sesame
  Japanese noodles with tahini
    dressing 91
  chickpea fritters with sesame
    sauce 94
shrimp
  bread risotto with seafood 56
Singapore fried noodles 92
sleepover party 69
slow-cooked beef with wine
  & olives 143
smörgasbord 114
smörkaker 155
soupe au pistou 76
soups
  bean soup with basil 76
  blueberry soup 12
  chicken soup with rice 24
  miso soup with beancurd 118
  pancake soup 156
  Ramadan lentil soup 90
  sleepover party 69
South Africa 95
  greens with peanuts 95
South-East Asia
  rice congee 14
  rice noodles with coconut
    milk & prawns 48
  see also Indonesia; Malaysia;
    Singapore; Thailand; Vietnam
Spain
  asparagus & potato tortilla 41
  chickpea stew with chorizo 55
  frittered calamares 36
  garlic chicken 82
  lemon barley water 25

olives, ham, cheese 33
pasta with pork 47
saffron rice with chicken &
  ham 72
spätzle mit kaiser 45
spinach
  chapatis with potato &
    spinach curry 111
  red lentils with spinach 20
  spinach & cheese parcels 131
squash
  quinoa & butternut squash 19
squid
  frittered calamares 36
su chow mein 92
supplí-al-telefono 66
Sweden
  meatballs with cream sauce 80
  Swedish butter-cookies 155
  Swedish cold table 114
sweet potato purée 16
Switzerland
  Dr Bircher's Swiss muesli 124

table manners
  in China 110
  in France 107
  in India 113
  in Japan 119
  in Morocco 117
  in Scandinavia 115
tahini
  Japanese noodles with tahini
    dressing 91
takeaway-style food 88–103
Thailand
  chicken rice with lemongrass
    & lime leaves 81
tofu *see* beancurd
tomato
  bread & tomato 20
  ham & tomato pasties 146
tortillas 43
  tortilla de asparagos trigueros
    141
treehouse picnic 73
Turkey
  potatoes & carrots 24
  spinach & cheese parcels 131
Tuscan winter minestrone 41

veal
  meatballs with cream sauce
    80
Vietnam
  rice-wrapper rolls 98

Welshcakes 153

yam *see* sweet potato
yassa 103
yellow rice with coconut milk
  51
yogurt
  polenta with yogurt 19

acknowledgements

Elisabeth says: I owe a long-standing debt of gratitude to my own children, Caspar, Francesca, Poppy and Honey, who were the initial recipients of my enthusiasm for taking the youngest members of the household on exotic gastronomic tours – even if the journey was only in the mind.

To my grandchildren – seven at the last count – the dedicatees of this book, who have had to put up with much culinary experimentation while the book was in preparation. To friends and colleagues – food-writers or child-carers (sometimes both) – for their willingness to share their knowledge.

To my agent, Abner Stein, without whom I wouldn't be a writer. To editor Caroline Taggart for unfailing support and enthusiasm. To designer Jenny Semple for tolerance and patience with the various artistic temperaments involved in the planning stages. And to my daughter-in-law and co-author, for her love and the pleasure we take in working together.

Frances says: I am thankful to Vanessa Holden for her quick design concepts – she's a genius.

To Ayesha Patel for introducing me to the joys of prop-rental companies, for her keen eye and sweet modern sensibility.

To Ngoc for taking such beautiful pictures, and her patience, energy and willingness to drink lukewarm tea.

To my mother-in-law for persevering with this project and for birthing her son, my husband – my love.

To Evelyn Rosario and Ziola Hidalgo for taking such good care of Sophie and Plum – for all their love and patience and for introducing the girls to La Comida and the joys of red beans and rice.

And to all our precious models, the children who have come to make this world a better place.

conversion tables

Weight (solids)				Volume (liquids)				Length	
15g	½oz	500g	1lb 2oz	250ml (¼ litre)	9fl oz	5mm	¼ inch
25g	1oz	600g	1lb 4oz	300ml	10fl oz	1cm	½ inch
40g	1½oz	700g	1lb 9oz		(½ pint)	5cm	2 inches
50g	1¾oz	750g	1lb 10oz	350ml	12fl oz	7cm	3 inches
75g	2¾oz	1kg	2lb 4oz	400ml	14fl oz	10cm	4 inches
100g	3½oz	1.2kg	2lb 12oz	425ml	15fl oz	15cm	6 inches
125g	4½oz	1.5kg	3lb 5oz		(¾ pint)	18cm	7 inches
150g	5½oz	2kg	4lb 8oz	450ml	16fl oz	20cm	8 inches
175g	6oz	2.25kg	5lb	500ml (½ litre)	18fl oz	24cm	10 inches
200g	7oz	2.5kg	5lb 8oz	600ml	20fl oz	28cm	11 inches
225g	8oz				(1 pint)	30 cm	12 inches
250g	9oz	**Volume (liquids)**		700ml	1¼ pints		
275g	9¾oz	15ml	½fl oz	750ml (¾litre)	1½ pints		
300g	10½oz	30ml	1fl oz	1 litre	1¾ pints		
325g	11½oz	50ml	2fl oz	1.2 litres	2 pints		
350g	12oz	100ml	3½fl oz	1.5 litres	2¾ pints		
400g	14oz	125ml	4fl oz	2 litres	3½ pints		
425g	15oz	150ml	5fl oz	2.5 litres	4½ pints		
450g	1lb		(¼ pint)	3 litres	5¼ pints		
		200ml	7fl oz	3kg	6lb 8oz		